SUPERIOR SERVANTS

The author as a baby with his amah, Ah Nui.

(Photograph S. K. Gaw)

SUPERIOR SERVANTS

THE LEGENDARY CANTONESE AMAHS
OF THE FAR EAST

KENNETH GAW

SINGAPORE
OXFORD UNIVERSITY PRESS
OXFORD NEW YORK
1991

Oxford University Press

Oxford New York Toronto
Delhi Bombay Calcutta Madras Karachi
Petaling Jaya Singapore Hong Kong Tokyo
Nairobi Dar es Salaam Cape Town
Melbourne Auckland
and associated companies in
Berlin Ibadan

Oxford is a trade mark of Oxford University Press

ISBN 0 19 588555 4

Printed in Malaysia by Percetakan Mun Sun Sdn. Bhd.,
Published by Oxford University Press Pte. Ltd.,
Unit 221, Ubi Avenue 4, Singapore 1440

For
Matthew, Kendal,
and Jamie

PREFACE

THIS book is neither a documentary history of Cantonese amahs nor an academic treatise on the subject. It simply reflects a personal interest. While they may well have been the finest of servants, I only remember them as friends and my memories of them are probably tinged with sentiment for a bygone age—when there were rubber trees to be tapped; when catapults made from *tembusu* trees were painstakingly seasoned over fires; when there were kite fights in the bluest of skies; when there were crystal-clear seas to swim in and unpolluted beaches to lie on—and most of all, when there were hawkers selling the most delicious foods passing by. Those were indeed the days! The amahs themselves? I remember them always being immaculately dressed in black and white—elegant, dignified, and caring. When Ah Woon, our baby amah, warned me that unless I ate up all my food I would come out in spots, I believed her completely and did as I was told. I felt safe with her around. Like many others, our amahs were an intrinsic part of our lives, familiar and reassuring.

Having known them all my life until I left to study and work abroad, I had always taken their presence for granted. It was, thus, quite a shock when I found, on a recent visit home, that they had all but vanished and that, surprisingly, so little was known about them. I also discovered that, with few exceptions, much of what had been written about them tended to be superficial or inaccurate and revealed little about them or their past.

Who were these women? From where did they come? What was it that made them exceptional? Were they indeed genuinely extraordinary or had they simply been exploited?

To answer these and other questions, I found it necessary first to delve into the past to ascertain the position of women in traditional Chinese society and life in China, particularly the Pearl River Delta, as well as to address the question of female emigration, and then to explore their lives in China and abroad, with comments from employers and their families to complete the picture.

I had not realized just how remarkable they were until I actually started writing. This book, therefore, is a belated tribute to these women who enriched the lives of so many families like ours and gave so much of themselves. I hope that it will go some way towards recognizing the fact that these superior servants were also very extraordinary women. I can well imagine their response to it—'Why do you want to write a book about us? We only did our jobs—we were nothing special.' They were.

London   KENNETH GAW
1988

ACKNOWLEDGEMENTS

EVEN a modest book such as this would not have been possible without the help of a considerable number of people. The amahs value their privacy, and had I not known them personally or been introduced by someone whom they knew and trusted, the interviews would have revealed little; and so, to the friends and relatives who helped with introductions and interviews, my thanks. I am grateful to the many employers, ex-employers, and their families for answering endless questions and for lending precious photographs from family albums. I wish to thank, in particular, my parents and my family for their considerable support. My mother also provided me with many useful details and my sister, Patricia, was indefatigable and generous in her help. My thanks go to Mary Ong for her assistance and interest, as well as to Tan Beng Luan of Singapore's Oral History Department. The help given to me by the library staff of the National University of Singapore and by William Schupbach of the Wellcome Institute Library in London is much appreciated, as are Fran Apelt's cartographic skills. Lim Bee Lum's contacts and her knowledge of life in Chinatown were invaluable, as was that of Tang Pui Yin, who also helped with interviews and translations. I am obliged to both of them, as I am to Choong Yu Pin and Lina Chiam for spending many tedious hours translating interviews. I am particularly indebted to Linda Neo for her indispensable assistance with all aspects of the book, from translations, Cantonese customs and terminology to proofreading and selection of photographs.

The Reverend Sek Fatt Kuan, president of the Tai Pei Old People's Home, has my thanks for allowing me to interview the residents there, and the Reverend Sek Yuen Sum, my eternal gratitude, for her considerable assistance, thoughtfulness, and unbounded enthusiasm.

These acknowledgements would not be complete without a very special thank-you to the remarkable amahs themselves for patiently sharing their fascinating experiences with me. In particular, I wish to mention Wan Yong Gui, Tang Ah Thye, Leong Siew Kee, and Tong Yuet Ching. Their indomitable and independent spirit, warmth, wisdom, and immense dignity will not be forgotten.

I reserve my ultimate thanks for my wife Polly, without whose help, advice, enthusiasm, and continual support, this book would still have only been just an interesting idea.

CONTENTS

PLATES

MAPS

INTRODUCTION

IN societies with extreme contrasts between rich and poor, domestic servants have long existed to attend to the needs of the better-off. This is as true in the late twentieth century as it was in Imperial China or Medieval Europe. The term 'servant', however, has largely fallen from use, particularly in the West, due to the social stigma attached to it. Until fairly recently, however, countless men and, especially, women worked as servants throughout the world. It was then an acceptable and even sought-after profession, particularly among the illiterate and unskilled. However, it is only in Third World countries that many are still widely employed as such.

The subject of this book is the Cantonese women from the province of Kwangtung (Guangdong) in South China who emigrated to the Far East, mainly in the 1930s, to work as domestic servants or amahs. They were a unique phenomenon. For many years they were an integral part of countless Chinese and expatriate, mainly British, homes in that region. Most of the women were single and from peasant backgrounds, yet they brought a standard of service and a degree of loyalty unequalled before or since.

There have been other devoted and excellent servants in the past. Some who come to mind are the black 'mammies' of North America's southern states and the nannies of Victorian England. The first exemplified warmth and the second, professionalism. The Cantonese amahs combined both.

There are parallels in the 1980s, notably the ubiquitous Filipinas who work as servants all over the world. The amahs were markedly different from this group as their character, expertise, and loyalty to the families they served made them incomparably superior. Moreover, while most of the Filipinas have had some education—some even hold degrees—virtually all the amahs were illiterate.

The women who became amahs emigrated chiefly to countries with a large Chinese population and usually with a sizeable number of British expatriates as well—the main ones being Hong

Kong, Singapore, and Malaya (Peninsular Malaysia). In Malaya, the amahs were primarily found in urban locations such as Penang, Kuala Lumpur, and Ipoh. Their presence, however, was probably most felt in Singapore. It is a small country and they were present in larger numbers than in Malaya. Although there were more Cantonese women in Malaya, fewer worked as amahs there due to the wider variety of work available, mainly in the tin and rubber industries.

Regardless of location, all the amahs enjoyed the same reputation as servants *par excellence*; but there was a subtle difference between the character of the amahs in Singapore and Malaya and those in Hong Kong. The first group was once described as being 'more bossy' than their Hong Kong counterparts—that is, they were more independent. This can be ascribed to the fact that while the amahs in Singapore and Malaya were far from home and without family support close at hand, many in Hong Kong had relatives both locally and in Canton (Guangzhou), the capital of Kwangtung. Canton is also the centre of the Pearl River Delta—the area from which the women came—and only about 130 km away.

The amahs' standard of service, once accepted as the norm, can perhaps best be appreciated by putting it into a contemporary context. Imagine the following advertisement appearing in the 'Situations Vacant' section of a contemporary newspaper:

Domestic Help Required: Live-in domestic servant required for family of four, two adults and two children.

Duties: Cooking, serving, marketing, cleaning, washing, ironing, general tidying-up, and other household duties as necessary.

Conditions of Work: Hours: 6 a.m–9 p.m. seven days/week. Two half days off/month.

Character: Must be hard-working, reliable, honest, discreet, and loyal. Cheerful disposition and resourcefulness an advantage.

Remuneration: $400–$600/month, depending on experience.

Would there be many applicants? It would be surprising if there were more than a handful and even more remarkable if there was even a single suitable applicant. Yet since their arrival, many thousands of Cantonese women have satisfactorily filled such positions. The servant who had to perform all the household tasks, as described, was known enigmatically as a *yat keok tek*—literally translated, 'one-leg-kick'.

All the amahs interviewed invariably burst knowingly into peals of laughter when asked if they had ever worked as a *yat keok tek*; most had. Their response is typical, not only of their sense of humour, but also of their stoicism—such a post in reality was extremely difficult and there was nothing even remotely amusing about the demanding job. The pay in the 1930s would have been between $5 and $10 per month, depending on experience. Admittedly, not every amah worked as a *yat keok tek*. There were those who only cooked, looked after children, or performed the household chores, but there were also some who actually did all the work, including minding the children.

While they were probably most famous in their jobs as baby amahs, i.e. 'nannies', they were equally valued for the impeccability of their household work and the standard of their culinary skills. But the quality that drew unqualified admiration, respect, and affection from all employers was their loyalty of service—many worked for families with total devotion till the day they retired.

It was not long after their arrival that they became an intrinsic part of life, particularly in Singapore. They were instantly recognizable in their characteristic dress of black, baggy, silky trousers and starched white cotton *samfoo* tops. This style of dress gave rise to the term, 'the black and white', by which they were widely known. With their neat 'uniform', good manners, and immaculate appearance—hair worn neatly either in a bun at the back of the head or in a single plait down their backs—they graced many a household.

From the 1930s to the 1970s, they were unrivalled as domestic servants. But their numbers have not been replaced and the few who are still working are in their late sixties or early seventies. And when they are gone, this remarkable group of women—'the black and white' Cantonese amahs—will cease to exist.

NOTES

Terminology. The majority of terms used are Cantonese. A glossary is provided at the end of the book, as are contemporary equivalents of place names, it being considered more appropriate to use names historically familiar to the period, e.g. 'Shun Tak' instead of 'Shunde' and 'Canton' rather than 'Guangzhou'.

Maps. For clarity, the map of the Pearl River Delta together with the inset map of Chinese provinces are shown with both contemporary and historical names, the latter being in parentheses.

Currency. The currency quoted throughout is the Singapore dollar. The following is a rough guide to average rates of exchange:

1930-1960:	US$1 =	Singapore $3.00.
	£1 =	Singapore $8.50.
1980s:	US$1 =	Singapore $2.20.
	£1 =	Singapore $3.50.

Entrance to village in the Pearl River Delta, Kwangtung, c.1870.

(Courtesy Wellcome Institute Library, London)

BACKGROUND

1 Yin and Yang symbol.

Traditionally depicted equal, but in practice Yang (male) was
always regarded as superior and Yin (female) as inferior.

I

'NOTHING ON EARTH IS HELD SO CHEAP'

A WOMAN'S LOT IN CHINA

THE attitude to women in China from time immemorial until well into the twentieth century was summed up in a single line by the poet Fu Hsuan in the third century BC: 'How sad it is to be a woman, nothing on earth is held so cheap.'

Women had no status independent of men, and marriage was the single most important objective in a girl's life. No Chinese father could commit a more serious sin of omission than to neglect his daughter's betrothal. Once married, the purpose of wives was to bear children or, more precisely, sons to carry on the family line.

The basis of Imperial China was the family and completely male-oriented, with filial piety being considered 'the root of all virtue'. Guiding every aspect of Chinese life for well over 2,000 years were the teachings of Confucius. The Confucian view was that 'women are human but lower than men' and 'a law of nature that woman should not be allowed any will of her own'. His philosophy, essentially practical in nature, was effectively the dominant one in China from around 500 BC to the beginning of the twentieth century—intended to create a stable social, ethical, and political order. To achieve this, however, required complete obedience on the part of the people and the creation of basic inviolable rules.

Of fundamental importance in this strategy was the ancient Chinese doctrine of the Yin and Yang forces of nature. Yang, the male force, was related to the elements of heaven, light, strength, activity, and goodness; while Yin, the female force, was associated with the elements of earth, darkness, weakness, passivity, and evil. In other words, Yang represented the desirable and Yin, the undesirable. In the traditional symbol of Yin and Yang, both are depicted equal, but in practice, however, Yang was superior and

3

Yin, inferior. This, then, was the traditional Chinese view of male and female.

There was no pleasure when girls were born. They were seen simply as being a drain on family resources. Common expressions such as 'Daughters are goods on which one loses one's capital' and 'It is better to raise geese than girls' underline the attitude towards girls. In other words, daughters were regarded as a poor investment. There was not only the cost of bringing them up but also, once married, they made no further contribution to their own family. To quote Lau Siew Yong: 'Daughters belong to other people when they grow up.' Even in the 1980s, this view is still held by some peasant communities in China.

There are few passages more painfully evocative of what it was like to be a woman in Imperial China than those contained in the chapter entitled 'No Name Woman' in Maxine Hong Kingston's *The Woman Warrior*. Life for women was incredibly restrictive. Their role in society was pre-ordained. While men could aspire to be scholars, adventurers, businessmen, or government officials, women could only be wives. Many Chinese writers wrote about the position of women and their role in the family and society. In relation to the entirely male-oriented society, the chief virtues of women were considered to be obedience, timidity, reticence, and adaptability. By far the most important was obedience.

Three rules of obedience shaped a woman's life from birth to death. Known as 'The Three Obeyings', the first decreed that an unmarried girl was to obey her father; the second, a married woman was to obey her husband; and the third, a widow was to obey her son.

The First Obeying. A father had total control over his daughter's life, including choice of marriage partner. His concern was that she should be properly trained in preparation for marriage and that she should 'earn her keep' until she was married. If she was unmarried and working, all her earnings went automatically to the head of the household—her father, or if he were no longer alive, the eldest brother or nearest male relative. Her chief role in the home was to help her mother.

As her intended role in life was only to be a wife and mother, it was considered a waste of time sending her to school; she would have been ineligible to sit the Civil Service Examinations anyway. Preparation for these examinations, open only to boys, was the chief function of schools. Consequently, girls were doomed to a

2 Examination Hall, Canton.
Civil Service Examinations, for which only boys were eligible,
were held in halls like this in centres throughout China.
(Courtesy Lim Kheng Chye)

life of illiteracy. Some wealthy fathers indulged themselves by engaging private tutors for their daughters, but these were the exception.

The Second Obeying. Provided she obeyed her husband, a married woman's position should have been more secure. This security, however, was not often achieved. First, she had to successfully practise the 'Four Virtues'. These concerned her moral behaviour, the correctness of her language, her dress, and her domestic expertise. Her moral behaviour had to be beyond reproach and she had to be soft-spoken to both her husband and mother-in-law and to do so in conciliatory tones. She also had to dress appropriately, that is, in clothes appropriate to her station. Finally, she had to be skilled in all household matters.

Secondly, and more importantly, she had to cope with the formidable figure of her mother-in-law. Despite her husband being the ostensible head of the household, it was invariably controlled by her mother-in-law. The relationship between mother- and daughter-in-law was always dominated by the older woman. This tradition was so deep-rooted that even Chinese families abroad once subscribed to it. Linda Neo, a Singapore journalist, recalls:

As a girl, I remember being told by my grandmother that her mother-in-law did everything to make her life a misery. She had to wait on her mother-in-law completely. If her mother-in-law wanted a cup of tea, for example, she would have to bring it to her and stand silently, either to the side or behind her, until she drank it. And naturally, after some time the tea would get cold, whereupon the older woman would taste it, complain that it was not fit to drink, fling the contents at her, and she would be told to make another cup. She had no choice but to do it—without argument.

The young wife was not even allowed to leave the house without her mother-in-law's permission. It was thus a very restricted and isolated life for her. Should her parents-in-law dislike her for any reason, they could insist that their son divorce her or send her home. As this would have been a terrible disgrace, most wives endured the most tyrannical of conditions. It is, perhaps, not surprising that many women waited for the day when they, in their turn, could have their revenge by taking it out on their future daughters-in-law.

It was not unknown for a wife to commit suicide as a result of the harsh treatment meted out to her by her husband and, particularly, her mother-in-law. Her position in society was such that she could not simply leave. Even her own family would not have accepted her back. Under such conditions, suicide often became her only way out. The tragic irony was that only when she was dead could her own family intervene and demand that various rites be performed, or that she be given an expensive funeral. Thus, she had more rights dead than alive. It is small wonder, then, that most of the amahs interviewed cited 'fear of the mother-in-law' and 'not wishing to belong to another family' as their main reasons for not getting married and why independence was so single-mindedly sought.

Some families attempted to avoid these potential difficulties by buying a young girl and bringing her up themselves with the specific intention of marrying her off to one of their sons when she was of age. This was known as the *sum-poh* form of marriage and although not widely practised, it was ingenious in principle and had certain practical advantages over the conventional system.

First, there was no upheaval in having to get used to the new bride or having to break her in. The 'daughter' simply became the daughter-in-law just as the 'mother' became the mother-in-law. Secondly, it was cheaper. With no other family involved, the marriage arrangements, particularly the marriage feast, could be simple, inexpensive affairs. Lastly, there was the security of knowing that, in their old age, the parents would be looked after by someone they knew well without having to rely on the word of a matchmaker regarding her qualities and character.

This arrangement was supposed to benefit the girl as well. She did not have to adjust to a new family on marriage nor have to cope with the dreaded mother-in-law. Also, as all marriages were matchmade and few girls ever knew their prospective husbands prior to marriage, she had the unique opportunity of knowing her future husband well. In reality, however, girls bought for this purpose were often treated more as servants than as daughters or future daughters-in-law and physically abused.

Once married, a young wife had more duties and fewer rights than she had in her own parents' home. To make matters worse, out of filial piety, a husband would normally side with his mother against his wife in any conflict between mother- and daughter-in-law. The wife's insecurity was compounded by the knowledge that her husband could simply divorce her on grounds known as 'The Seven Outs'. These included barrenness, disobeying or neglecting his parents, adultery or wanton conduct, and jealousy. The other three were talkativeness, having a repulsive disease, and theft.

7

Of the 'Seven Outs', the most feared was that of barrenness, as it was only by producing a son that she could consolidate her position and be fully accepted as a member of his family, i.e. she would be connected to it via her son.

There were, however, conditions known as 'The Three Reasons' on which she could not be divorced. These were: mourning for her parents-in-law for three years after their deaths; her husband's family becoming wealthy after she married into it; and a surprisingly compassionate third reason—if she had no family to return to.

There were no grounds upon which she could divorce her husband. Consequently, divorce became exclusively the husband's privilege. Furthermore, due to the lack of job opportunities and her poor education, divorce remained a futile option. There were few ways in which she could earn a living aside from being a prostitute, matchmaker, or nun. It was also socially frowned upon, even by members of her own family. Hence, divorces did not occur.

Divorce by 'mutual consent' was possible, but only with the agreement of the respective families and the approval of the state, which had to be convinced that the man's family would suffer if the marriage continued. Such divorces, too, were rare.

The extreme precariousness of the wife's position was further emphasized by the practice of allowing the husband to sell or pawn his wife in times of hardship. This happened despite being illegal as well as contravening Chinese moral teachings. A woman was thus simply treated as a chattel. It was noted in Hugh D. R. Baker's *Chinese Family and Kinship* that in the nineteenth century, pawning of wives among the lower and middle classes of society was widespread in the provinces of Hunan, Chekiang (Zhejiang), Kiangsu (Jiangsu), and Anhwei (Anhui) due to poverty. Even mothers with children were pawned. And there was at least one reported case of a man selling his wife simply because he had been angry with her for visiting her own family too frequently.

The Third Obeying. A widow was entirely dependent on her son as all her husband's money and property would be left to him and she would be left nothing. But while she would acknowledge her son as head of the household, he would, out of filial piety, defer to her in matters of practical importance such as the running of the household and in the choice of a wife. And should he be married, he would usually side with his mother in any disagreement between his wife and his mother. For the same reason, it would have been unthinkable for him to neglect his mother's well-being or to turn her out, regardless of how she behaved. She was a highly influential figure in his life.

Thus, a widow with a son and no male adult relatives on her husband's side was in a particularly powerful position. But if she had no son, not only would she never be properly accepted as a member of that family but, more importantly, she could not be an ancestress, i.e. her soul would have no means of support after her death. With a son, her existence after death was secure and she became as immortal as her husband. Bearing a son was, therefore, of great earthly as well as spiritual importance and explains why the inability to produce a son was so greatly feared.

From the time of Confucius, there existed a list of what were considered the most significant and important relationships in society, known as 'The Five Human Relationships'. In descending order of importance, these were: ruler/minister, father/son, elder brother/younger brother, husband/wife, and friend/friend. With the exception of the last named, all indicated superior/inferior relationships as well. It clearly delineated the place of women in Chinese society. Mothers and daughters had no place on this list. The only position of any importance a woman could occupy was when she became a wife, although she was still inferior to her husband. The real strength of her position, however, was dependent on her producing a son.

Nothing, perhaps, demonstrated the inferior status of Chinese women more dramatically than the painful and horrific practice, unique to Chinese women, of footbinding. These deformed feet were euphemistically called 'lotus' or 'lily' feet. Girls had their feet bound when they were around five years old, when their bones were already well formed. The practice was widely known but seldom described. Binding was done with strips of strong cotton, about 1.5 m long and 18 cm wide. These were wound over and over the four toes, leaving only the big toe free, until eventually the toe bones were broken and they lay as flat as possible beneath the sole. The strips were drawn so tightly round the heel that it caused the arch bone to curve. It was excruciatingly painful and took about two years before the pain disappeared, but the custom was so entrenched that mothers continued to inflict it on their daughters despite the agonies they themselves had suffered. There was also the danger of infection and gangrene and the possible loss of life. Walking was always difficult and their health

3 Bound feet: The fashionable image.
Girls had their feet bound from the age of five.
(Courtesy Lim Kheng Chye)

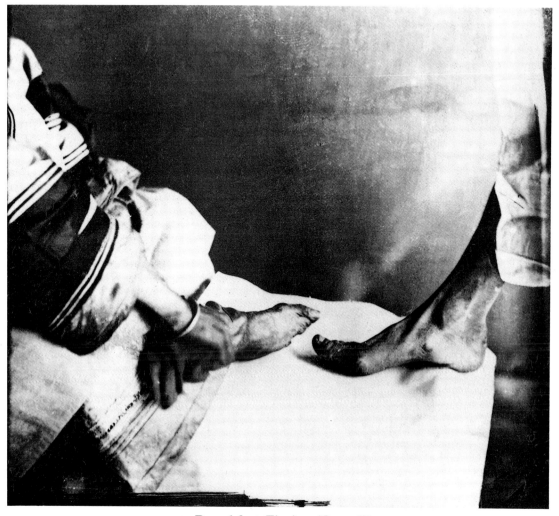

4 Bound feet: The horrific reality.
An 1871 photograph showing the comparison between a bound and
deformed foot, and a natural one.
(Courtesy Wellcome Institute Library, London)

inevitably suffered through poor deportment, bad circulation, and lack of exercise.

What was the reason for this horrendous practice? There was no religious significance. It was simply a social custom apparently started around AD 970 by Emperor Li Yu, who reputedly had a gold pedestal built in the shape of a lotus flower and had one of his concubines dance on it with feet tightly bound in silk—hence the term 'lotus feet'.

Bound feet became tremendously popular thereafter. They were supposed to look dainty and beautiful, and the gait of a woman with bound feet was apparently of considerable sexual appeal to men. It became a sign of breeding to have bound feet. All but the poorest families had the feet of their daughters bound as they believed it would improve their marriage prospects. A woman with normal feet was considered unattractive and indicated that she belonged to the labouring or coolie class. It reached the stage that matchmakers were often not asked about the prospective bride's beauty but how small her feet were. And it was regarded as adequate grounds for calling off the marriage if, at the betrothal ceremony, the husband-to-be discovered that his intended wife's feet were larger than he had been led to believe.

In some provinces, after the marriage ceremony, the wife would be taken around the village in a cart so that the villagers could see her and it was a considerable source of embarrassment if her feet were not small enough. The perfect bound foot was supposed to be no more than 8 cm or about 3 inches; in other words, less than *half* the size of a normal Chinese female foot, which was about 20 cm.

Regardless of the popularity of the custom, there was a practical reality in the practice of footbinding. Bound feet made travelling even short distances painful. By restricting women to the home, it effectively enforced fidelity and eliminated any possible independence. Being 'housebound' had an entirely different meaning then. The irony was that women were not only willing participants but also became the staunchest supporters of the practice, akin, perhaps, to the passion for the uncomfortable wasp-waist or stiletto heels in the West.

Footbinding was practised throughout China with few exceptions. These included poor families who needed their womenfolk to work in the fields and the Manchus, who considered it barbaric but were unable to put a stop to it as it was such an entrenched custom. It was least popular amongst the Hakkas and the people in the south, notably the natives of Fukien (Fujian) and especially Kwangtung. Although officially abolished by the Republican government in 1911, footbinding persisted well into the twentieth century, with cases reported in remote provinces even after the Communist take-over in 1949.

Conditions in China were frequently so severe that many children were born into families unable to sustain them. Female infanticide was a common solution. The poor accepted the practice as an essential—and almost legitimate—means of maintaining their minimal standard of living. Some girl babies were smothered while others were buried alive, but drowning or 'turning their faces into the mud' were the most common methods. It was estimated by Christian missionaries in Kwangtung in the nineteenth century that only one in three females was allowed to live in certain districts. The harsh economic conditions and prevalent social attitude resulted in the killing of female infants continuing right into the twentieth century. In *Chinese Women Speak*, Dymphna Cusack wrote about life in the 1920s in Chekiang Province. Women were held in such low regard and conditions so harsh that if a mother bore three girls, the third would probably be killed despite any affection she had for the child. The irony of the situation was that this tragic practice together with the high mortality rate in childhood and early adult life often brought about a shortage of women, and parents were forced to go far afield to purchase wives for their sons.

There was, however, one part of China where daughters were valued—the silk-producing district of Shun Tak (Shunde) in the Pearl River Delta region of Kwangtung. Agnes Smedley, in *China Correspondent*, noted during her travels in China in the 1930s, that this was the only place in the country where the birth of a girl was welcomed—for daughters here, instead of being a drain on family resources, were often the main support of their families.

Poverty-stricken parents unwilling or unable to kill their daughters often abandoned them in prominent places in the towns or on the doorsteps of wealthy households, in the hope that they would be taken in. Orphanages run by Christian missionaries in the nineteenth century were a last resort, probably because the Chinese still regarded foreigners as inferior barbarians.

Children, especially girls, were often sold or exchanged for food. There was a ready market for girls sold as servants, prostitutes, or concubines. It was an accepted Chinese custom to sell daughters in times of hardship. A girl sold to be a servant was known as a *mui tsai*. She would literally be the property of the person who bought her—'like a slave'. Choong Hup Yee recalls that an uncle of hers in the 1920s 'sold one of his daughters, about five or six, as a *mui tsai* to a rich family when conditions were bad'.

There were established customs for girls sold as *mui tsai*. It was understood that in return for doing the household chores, she was to be properly looked after by her employer and be regarded as a member of the family, albeit a minor one—hence the term *mui tsai*, which means 'little younger sister'. It was also understood that she was to be married off when she was of age (about eighteen) at the expense of her employer. Some became their master's concubine. It was also accepted that she could be bought back by her parents on repayment of any monies received, though this rarely happened. Others were transferred as a pledge for a loan and their services were regarded as interest until the loan was repaid. To ensure that the girl was being well treated, her parents were supposed to check on her occasionally.

The practice had some merit, at least in principle, as the girl would have been sold not only to benefit the family but also to give her a better start in life than she would have had in the impoverished family home. Supporters of the system, which included many influential Chinese businessmen in Hong Kong, maintained that it was 'an act of charity' as it helped both the girls and their families. In reality, however, it was open to widespread abuse, particularly when parents were unable to check on their daughters' well-being. This inevitably happened when employers lived far away or travelled abroad. The exploitation of girls reached its height in the latter part of the nineteenth century when there was an insatiable demand for Chinese girls and women in the almost totally male Chinese population of the Nanyang, i.e. South-East Asia. The problem was even worse in Hong Kong, where access from the Pearl River Delta was easy and the *mui tsai* system was widely accepted.

Many girls allegedly bought as *mui tsai* often ended up as singing girls, prostitutes, or concubines. Others were treated as domestic slaves and often sexually and physically exploited. They were, in the main, treated very badly and thus the endearing term *mui tsai*—'little younger sister'—was extremely euphemistic. One irony, however, was that a *mui tsai* often had more freedom than her mistress: she could leave the house to shop or to run errands, while her mistress, restricted to the house by social convention, could not.

The abuses the *mui tsai* were subjected to were well known to

5 A *mui tsai*.
In this *c.*1868 picture taken in Kwangtung, she is shown on her
way to market, ironically 'enjoying more freedom in going
abroad than does the mistress'.
(Courtesy Wellcome Institute Library, London)

the British authorities but difficult to eliminate. The Anti-Mui Tsai Society in Hong Kong, formed largely of Chinese Christians with the backing of the Christian Churches, pressed for total abolition in a widely publicized unequivocal manifesto declaring that: the system contravened humanitarian principles as it allowed human beings to be treated as commercial property; it was immoral as it allowed girls to be sexually exploited or physically tortured by their masters; it harmed the international prestige of the Chinese race and ran against the evolutionary progress of society in its denial of equal rights. It concluded by saying that it was 'essentially unbiblical'. The Society's efforts caused Winston Churchill, then Secretary of State for the Colonies, to cable Hong Kong's Governor, Sir Reginald Stubbs, in 1922 to put an end to 'female child slavery'.

Aware of the opposition of the powerful Chinese lobby against total abolition, Stubbs chose a middle path. The Female Service Ordinance of 1923 stated that no new *mui tsai* were to be engaged and all existing ones registered. It was a feeble attempt. By the end of 1927, out of an estimated 12,000 *mui tsai*, just over 4,000 had been registered. The Ordinance was tightened in 1929, but the problem remained unresolved.

Despite the more far-reaching Mui Tsai Bill of 1932, conditions did not appreciably improve until 1937, when a commission was set up to investigate the *mui tsai* in Hong Kong and Malaya. It produced a lengthy report that ended with recommendations on improving the situation. It was, however, the changing conditions and attitudes after the Second World War that eventually caused the demise of the system. Nevertheless, the selling of daughters in times of privation was still so ingrained that H. J. Lethbridge, in his *Hong Kong: Stability and Change*, noted an item in the *South China Morning Post* on 16 September 1971 which reported that two girls, aged six and eleven, had been sold by their parents in the New Territories to a housewife as domestic servants. The elder was 'leased' for a period of four years for HK$6,000 and the younger sold for life for HK$2,800.

It is, perhaps, worth noting that not all *mui tsai* were exploited. The Lo family in Hong Kong had a *mui tsai* who worked for them until they emigrated to North America. She was married off and had a daughter but later returned to work for the family because 'her family life was poor'. When the family left, she retired and went to live in a Vegetarian House at their expense. They remitted funds annually for her support until her death in 1987.

Thus, for thousands of years, the phrase 'nothing on earth is held so cheap' all too accurately described the status of women in Chinese society. Females were subjected to a wide range of abuses and their lowly status was such that they were invariably sacrificed in times of hardship. It is worth remembering that almost all these abuses were still much in evidence in the early years of the twentieth century, when most of the amahs interviewed were born, and China, once the most advanced civilization on earth, was no longer the 'centre of the world'.

6   A group of starving peasants in Kwangsi Province, 1903.

Sights like this were once common in China, a result of natural
disasters, war, corruption, and complacency.
(Courtesy Hong Kong Government)

2

GREAT UPHEAVALS; LITTLE CHANGES

IN the early years of the twentieth century, China was undergoing a period of traumatic change. The Manchu Dynasty was collapsing and China discovered that it was no longer the all-powerful 'Middle Kingdom'. The seriousness of the situation was expressed by the Dowager Empress Tz'u Hsi in January 1901 when she stated that China needed to 'reform completely'. A brief look at the events that brought the mighty Chinese Empire to this painful position will help to put things in perspective and underline conditions existing at the start of the twentieth century.

First, there were its defeats by the Western powers in the Opium War of 1839-42 and in the Arrow War of 1858-60, resulting in China having to open all its ports to foreign trade and being forced to accept unequal treaties with conditions such as trading at terms substantially advantageous to the West. Various foreign nations were also granted territorial rights. This eventually led to a separate system of laws and jurisdiction within the foreign concessions, which meant exemption from Chinese law and taxes. The role of opium, which the British deliberately exploited, cannot be too heavily stressed. It had a debilitating influence on the population, as well as a profound effect on the economy. Together with other countries, the British insisted that the opium be paid for in silver, the monetary standard of the country. This outflow of silver greatly weakened the economy. Corrupt Chinese officials also benefited from this lucrative trade.

The cost of living soared, making life even more difficult for the exploited, hard-pressed peasants, already subject to nature's catastrophes of drought, flood, and famine. The combination of all these conditions led to various local revolts, culminating in the monumental uprising known as the Taiping Rebellion of 1850-64. It was a devastating conflict with an estimated 25,000,000 deaths—about half the total number killed in the Second World War. Although enjoying widespread popularity, it eventually failed due to the Taipings' own serious internal strife and the help that the Manchus received from the Westerners, who feared that they would lose all the considerable benefits they had hitherto enjoyed if the Manchus were overthrown.

The rebellion was notable not only because of its sheer scale but also for its intended revolutionary reforms. These included: Common Property—private ownership was to be abolished; Land Reform—land was to be distributed fairly among the population with men and women being treated equally and children under the age of sixteen getting half the amount; Treatment of Foreigners—due to their Christian influence, the Taipings regarded all people as equal and that the Chinese were not 'the chosen people'; Position of Women—women were to be treated the same as men. In many ways, this last was the most radical of their planned reforms. This equality of treatment would have been completely unprecedented, deviating from thousands of years of inviolable tradition.

Women were to be allowed to take state examinations, from which they had previously been barred, as well as hold civil and military office. This would, of course, have necessitated the education of girls, thus equipping them for occupations other than the traditional ones as wives, concubines, mistresses, matchmakers, or nuns. The result would have given women economic freedom—and independence.

Other reforms planned included marriage arrangements and the care of women. Although there was still emphasis on daughters marrying, the choice of partner was left to the individuals themselves and not to the customary financial arrangements organized by matchmakers. Women and girls who did not have the support and protection of male family members, either by design or accident, were to be specially cared for. Their Christian influence made monogamy obligatory. Female abuses such as footbinding and prostitution were strictly forbidden and white slavery and rape punishable by death.

Had the Taipings been successful and these reforms put into practice, it would have been an astronomical leap forward in the emancipation of Chinese women. Nevertheless, the seeds for future reform were sown; but it was not until almost fifty years later that some of the proposals were adopted by Sun Yat Sen and later by the Communists as well.

Perhaps the most significant event in the downfall of the

Manchus was the Sino-Japanese War of 1894. China had always considered itself culturally and spiritually superior to the West and hence even though its defeats in the Opium and Arrow Wars were shattering, it was nothing like the humiliation it suffered on losing to its former vassal, Japan, in 1894. How could it possibly be defeated by a country with a similar cultural and spiritual background to its own? The unthinkable had happened. It made the Chinese question that which had made them supreme for so long—tradition and the Confucian system.

The final blow to the Manchus was the crushing of the Boxer Rebellion of 1900 by the West. This was a last attempt to rid China of foreigners and supported by no less a personage than the Dowager Empress herself. The Boxers were Chinese peasant bands who were so called because they practised Chinese boxing and whose war-cry was 'Protect the Ching. Exterminate the foreign devils.' This attracted the support of many Manchu princes and high officials. In the early stages, however, the Boxers were actually anti-dynastic and their slogan then was 'Overthrow the Ching and expel the barbarians.' The target of their original hatred, however, were the Christian churches, which often displayed great intolerance towards the people, such as their opposition to the ancient tradition of ancestor-worship. This hatred eventually culminated in their chief aim of wanting to expel all foreigners and kill Christian converts.

Given that the Rebellion enjoyed considerable support from the highest in the land, it was a considerable 'loss of face' for the Manchus when the Boxers were defeated in the summer of 1900. A significant item in the very exacting terms dictated by the West was the establishment of a Ministry of Foreign Affairs which was to enjoy a higher rank than other ministries. This enhanced status given to foreign relations marked a reversal of the traditional attitude towards 'inferior barbarians'.

Although the Manchus tried to introduce changes, it was too late. Sun Yat Sen and his followers had already begun 'preaching treason in lands across the seas' to Chinese emigrants abroad and encouraging them to demonstrate their opposition to the Manchus, which they did by cutting their queues. Soon, the message was preached in China itself with Canton being at the centre of the revolutionary movement. By then, the Manchus were so weak that it was only a matter of time before they were finally overthrown in the Republican Revolution of 1911.

Many reforms were undertaken by the new government,

7 Little changes.
Despite the overthrow of the Manchus in 1911, little had changed.
Two starving children of indeterminate age being fed by a
relief worker. Early twentieth century.
(Courtesy Hong Kong Government)

including the banning of footbinding and the encouragement of women as wage-earners; but it was a painfully slow task—inertia created through several millennia is not conducive to rapid change. Sun Yat Sen was under no illusion of the difficulties facing his new government. He acknowledged this in a speech on the difficulties ahead and the sacrifices to be made, to students of Hongkong University some twelve years later in February 1923. These difficulties were seemingly insurmountable. The late celebrated American journalist, Edgar Snow, wrote a moving account of the famine following the Great Drought of 1929 which devastated a fourth of China and killed over five million people. He was stunned by the horrific scenes of starvation he saw but even more shocked by the fact that in many towns there were rich men, rice hoarders, money-lenders, and landlords, all profiteering enormously. And in cities, there were thousands of tons of grain which could not be sent to the starving because the army and bureaucracy would not allow trains to be used to transport the food. Little had changed in China.

The agricultural system, backbone of the economy, desperately needed modernization. Transportation and communication systems were archaic. There were continuing and damaging inter-provincial conflicts and the country was still suffering from widespread corruption and complacency. Finally, there were the regular scourges of drought, flood, and famine. China was in an appalling state.

After centuries of corrupt government and strict Confucian tradition, it was impossible for China to adapt rapidly to changing conditions elsewhere and to 'reform completely', as Tz'u Hsi had urged in 1901. This then was the China in which the amahs grew up.

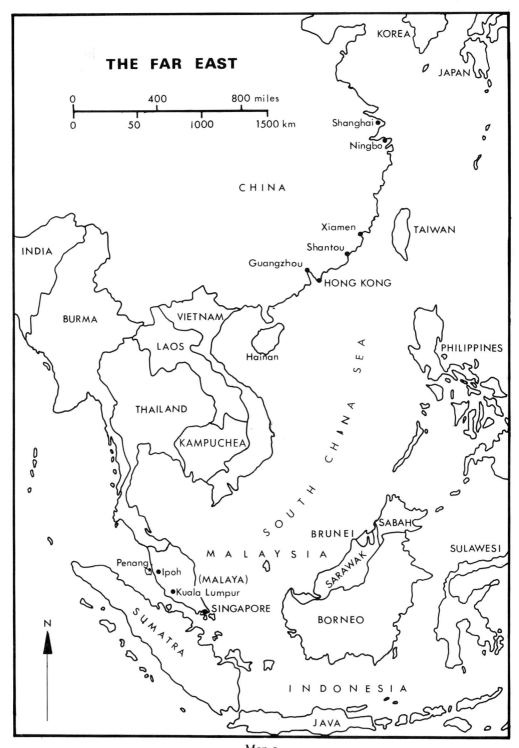

Map 1

3

SILKWORMS AND RICE

THE Cantonese amahs came from an agricultural area of Kwang-tung Province in the south-east known as the Pearl River Delta into which flow the East River (Dongjiang), the West River (Xijiang), and the North River (Beijiang). Roughly 11 000 square kilometres in area, the delta is crossed by a network of streams and rivers with some outlying hills. It is renowned for its production of silk and as a rice-growing area. Due to the fertility of the soil, it supports an extraordinary density of population. Rice is cropped twice a year but sweet potatoes and rape-seed are also important. There are many subsidiary crops—tobacco in the west, jute in the east, as well as tea, sugar-cane, and a variety of tropical fruit. Fish is plentiful and reared locally in ponds.

Almost all the amahs came from this simple peasant background and worked locally. Some went to Canton, the provincial capital, to work as domestics. Others occasionally went there to trade and shop. The only time when most ventured there was to use it as a springboard for travel to Hong Kong and abroad when emigrating.

The amahs came predominantly from two districts—Shun Tak and Tung Koon (Dongguan)—as well as from Sam Sui (Sanshui) (lower), Nam Hoi (Nanhai), Poon Yue (Panyu), San Wui (Xin-hui), and Chong San (Zhongshan), amongst others. Shun Tak, Nam Hoi, and lower Sam Sui districts were mainly involved in the silk industry—the breeding of silkworms and the weaving of silk. Upper Sam Sui, incidentally, was the home of that other extraordinary breed of Cantonese woman—the hardy red-hatted *samsui* building labourer—and now, like the Cantonese amah, virtually non-existent. The other districts grew rice as well as other crops. There were also small cottage industries involved in the making of hats, fans, baskets, string and rope.

When the silk industry declined as a result of the mass production of synthetic silk or rayon in Japan and elsewhere, land was converted from the growing of mulberry bushes to sugar-

25

8   Pearl River, Kwangtung, c.1870.

The Pearl River Delta—home of the amahs and famed for its
production of silk and rice.

(Courtesy Wellcome Institute Library, London)

cane, tobacco, and other more profitable cash crops. Although a very fertile area, it was, like many other parts of China, beset by a range of natural disasters such as floods, typhoons and locusts. Wan Yong Gui, from Tung Koon, gives a detailed account of life in the 1920s:

Our place was poor. There was starvation after every flood. Quite often, there were floods. If the rice crops were destroyed, we starved. Flooding during flowering of the grain was most disastrous. Nothing was left after that. Insects were another scourge. They were colourful—red, green, yellow, and black. They would destroy the tender shoots; every shoot would be eaten. Nothing would be left for humans that year. It was a puzzle where they came from. Counter-measures were taken, but not with modern methods such as spraying with insecticides. There wasn't any then. It is different now. That was how China was then and living was very tough. These natural disasters were most fearful. Another was destruction by mice. Again, their origin was a puzzle. They bit the shoots. The destruction by insects or mice would happen every five to six years. Sometimes after four years. It was bound to happen.

Not all, however, was doom and gloom. She recalls:

When there was a good harvest, nothing needed to be bought except salted fish, cooking oil, and sugar. Those who planted sugar-cane could make their own sugar. Every village had its lychee and longan orchards. Mainly for our own consumption but we also engaged in spot sales. Some were given away as presents. Dry, open land was the most suitable.

If they were to be sold, the owner of the orchard was usually approached by fruit buyers for the whole crop for the season. By the first of the third moon, these buyers would come to view the orchards if there wasn't any rain. Nobody would come if it rained, for the flowers would have been destroyed. These flowers were white and in bunches. The buyers would bid only if there were flowers on the trees. Normally, they would bid for the whole crop and the owner just kept a few bunches for himself. What a sight when the lychee ripened! The whole place was red in colour!

The traditional Chinese calendar is based on the lunar year, in contrast to the Western solar year calendar. The land was sometimes owned by the families themselves, but more usually, it was rented and it was common practice for the farmer to offer a proportion of the produce in lieu of rent. It was always the ambition of every farmer to own land but this was rarely possible due to poor harvests or, even worse, no harvests at all. Earning a good and steady income from land was very difficult. Money remitted home by amahs abroad was often used to buy land and buffaloes and to build houses—in that order. The land was never left idle and nothing ever went to waste. She continues:

Rice was planted in the twelfth moon and harvested in the third, followed by jute. The stem of the jute was used as firewood or, after cleaning and grinding, could be made into string. Jute was harvested in the fourth moon and grain or rice followed. Buffaloes were used to till the land. This crop of grain or rice could be harvested by the tenth moon.

The toughness of farm life led, amongst other things, to the attitude that nothing should be wasted. This attitude was exemplified in silkworm farming. Excrement left by the worms was used to fertilize the fields and to feed the fish. Even human faeces was used as manure. 'Ash from the stove was used to cover the faeces to kill the stench! This human faeces was then used as fertilizer after treatment with the ashes.'

Farm work was done by the adult males in the household with the wives helping after household chores were completed. Girls helped their mothers. By the age of four or five, they were expected to look after their younger siblings. By seven or eight, they had to help their mothers with the household chores—fetching, carrying, and cleaning—together with simple farm tasks such as looking after the buffaloes and gathering fuel. By their teens, they would be helping with the cooking as well as having to perform more arduous work such as treading the water-wheel. They also had to care for the farmyard animals and tend the vegetables. In short, they were involved in all domestic tasks, thus preparing them for their later roles as wives.

By contrast, boys did very little. Their main duty was to attend school and to study. They did not have specific chores and usually did not help in the fields till they were in their teens. Their education was restricted to the learning of the Chinese classics. Schools were usually organized by the village or clan and were fee-paying. If parents were unable to pay cash, which often happened, they would pay the teachers in rice or other produce. Says Lui Wai Foon wistfully, 'For girls, there was no time to play.' She even had to subsidize the family income by helping to make string for *lup cheong* (Chinese sausages) from the age of four. She got about 60 cents for a *kati* (about 0.6 kg) of string. Boys, on the other hand, could relax once they had completed their day's studies. Ow Ah Tim confirms, 'Sons never helped. They could play.'

9 Girls worked from an early age.

In this detail taken from an early twentieth-century postcard,
a young girl is shown carrying her baby brother
not much smaller than herself.
(Courtesy Lim Kheng Chye)

10 Boys relaxing in a river, *c.*1870.
'Sons never helped. They could play.'
(Courtesy Wellcome Institute Library, London)

In the silk-producing districts of Shun Tak, lower Sam Sui, and Nam Hoi, land was used for cultivating mulberry bushes, the leaves of which were fed to the silkworms. This was a cottage industry with individual families having their own plots of land and rearing the silkworms indoors. They sold the silk cocoons at the markets to buyers from the big towns. Leong Ah Hoe, from Nam Hoi, provides a fascinating account of the industry, starting with the purchase of the silkworm eggs:

I went to the market to buy the silkworm eggs which came in pieces of paper roughly a foot square [25 cm square]. I kept the eggs in a small basket and, after some time, the eggs hatched and the silkworms were born. Each was as fine as a strand of hair.

When I returned home, I would pluck mulberry leaves and cut them into very small pieces and spread the cut-up leaves over the silkworms. After the silkworms had eaten, they excreted on the piece of paper. Then the soiled paper would be removed and replaced by a fresh one.

The basket where the silkworms slept must be kept very clean, without a speck of dust. If not, ants would come and bite the silkworms and they would not spin silk. There must be fresh air. Once they were fully grown, they would weave a cocoon of silk around themselves. If the silkworms were healthy, they would weave very nice cocoons, smooth and thick. If they were weak, the cocoons would appear broken and thin. If the cocoons were properly woven, they could be sold at the market, but if not, no one would buy them.

Silkworms were raised six times a year, starting in February and stopping around August. They could not be bred after August as the climate would start getting cold from September and the mulberry bushes stopped growing leaves.

Houses were usually single-storey dwellings and accommodation was usually basic and cramped. A typical house had one or two bedrooms, a hall which also doubled as sitting room and bedroom, a kitchen, and a bathroom. Toilets were outdoor and shared with other houses. Lui Wai Foon describes the lighting conditions: 'The windows did not have any glass and were small. It was dark inside the house and we had an airwell to make the house lighter.' The hall also contained the altar. Favourite deities were Kwan Yin, the Goddess of Mercy; the Kitchen God; the Monkey God; and Kuan Ti, the God of War. The kitchen was simple, usually with a single stove fuelled by dried grass, flax stems, wood, or charcoal. Furniture was minimal, with a table, some stools and, occasionally, a few hard-backed wooden chairs. Clothing was as basic: besides their work clothes, they usually had only a better set of clothes, reserved for special occasions.

11 Kwangtung family, c.1870
'Furniture was minimal ... clothing was basic.'
(Courtesy Wellcome Institute Library, London)

12 Kwangtung farm, c.1870.

Even in the 1930s, conditions in rural areas were much the same
as when this photograph was taken.

(Courtesy Wellcome Institute Library, London)

There were no taps. Water for the household had to be fetched in buckets from the river, pond, or well, and bathing was simple. 'We bathed by jumping into the water with our clothes on and in cold weather we did warm mopping.' The outdoor toilets were shared by a group or row of houses. 'The toilet was far away from the house. It was a brick shed with a roof made of wooden planks and divided into two, one for the males, the other for females, and a few wooden boards to squat on.' There was no electricity either. In the evenings, lighting was provided by candles, oil-lamps, or pressure lamps. Due to the lack of external lighting or street lamps, Wan Yong Gui laughingly recalls that 'Going to the toilet at night was scary. By ten o'clock, everyone was in bed. No midnight strollers!'

Entertainment and recreational activities were also very limited. The highlight of any occasion was the visit of a travelling theatre or operatic troupe. The performances were always based on classical legends and stories such as 'The Water Margin', 'Romance of the Three Kingdoms', or 'A Dream of Red Mansions', with young men playing the women's roles, it being considered unseemly for women to be seen on stage. Actors were traditionally considered to be of low social class—'on a level with barbers'—and ineligible to sit the state examinations: in other words, on a par with women.

These visits were especially important for the girls and women. First, the performances were their only escape from a life of unremitting drudgery. Women in traditional Chinese theatre or opera are often featured as princesses or heroines performing exciting and great deeds. These adventures, however, were still restricted to women taking on male roles—women warriors. They were never portrayed as noble, independent women in their own right. Secondly, as the womenfolk were illiterate, the performances were their chief, if not their only, means of learning about Chinese history. It also explains why traditional Cantonese opera, whether performed in the street or on television, was the most popular form of entertainment for the amahs in later years. These events were also welcome distractions for the men.

The main occasions for celebration were the traditional Chinese festivals such as the Chinese New Year, the Festival of the Hungry Ghosts, and the Mid-autumn Festival. More routine forms of social recreation such as frequenting tea-houses and listening to story-tellers were strictly only for men, the women's place being in the home. In fact, the division between the sexes was so sharp that after early childhood, girls and boys neither played together nor met in any recognized and proper way. The men were less affected as they were not restricted to the home but the only women with whom they could normally mix freely were prostitutes. During hot summers, girls had a slightly easier life, with swimming and bathing in the river.

Food in peasant villages was simple, comprising rice and vegetables with a little meat or fish. Vegetables used were local and seasonal:

Each month, we ate a different type of vegetable. In January, we planted long beans; in February and March, we ate long beans, brinjal, and salted vegetables. July and August were good for taro. During August and September, sweet potatoes grew in abundance. Leaf mustard and white cabbage were plentiful in December. Garlic, ginger, and onions grew almost all the year round. (Leong Ah Hoe.)

Eggs were a popular item, as were chickens, duck, and pork, when conditions were good; otherwise, the diet was restricted. Fresh-water fish and prawns were a welcome addition to the menu. Lui Wai Foon recalls fondly, 'When the sun came out after it had rained heavily for a long time, the prawns would jump up in the air and were easily caught.' The fish in the ponds were auctioned off annually. She remembers it being a 'good life'.

For most of the others, this was not the case. If they were not struck by natural disasters, they were victims of war, local as well as international. Leong Ah Hoe recollects:

The people from Kwangtung and Kwangsi were at war. They had fought for many years and caused chaos in our village. There wasn't enough to eat, yet the soldiers stole from us. They killed our chickens and pigs. They came and took everything from our homes. Although none of the men in the village were called upon to fight, some were forced to be pack-bearers and had to go with the soldiers. Few ever returned.

Life, then, was frequently as hard in the Pearl River Delta as it was in other parts of the land, and subject to the same natural and man-made disasters. Similarly, the same attitudes towards women as inferior human beings prevailed there as elsewhere. Yet, the women of this region managed to achieve a degree of independence unknown anywhere else in China.

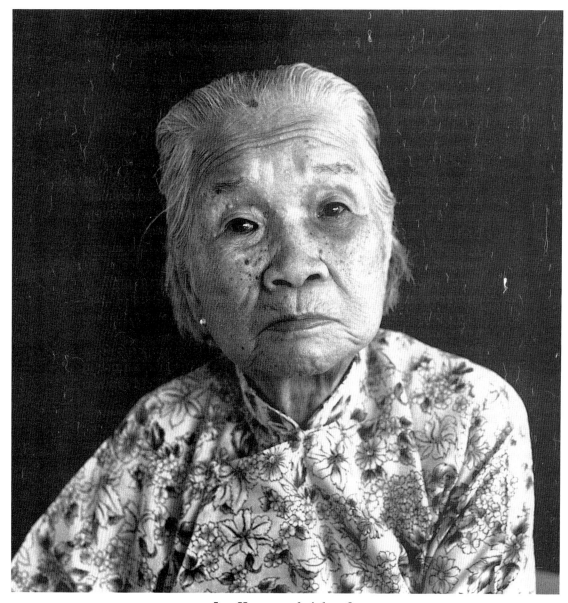

13 Lee Heng, aged eighty-four.

'I enjoy independence. I earn my own money.
I use my own money. Nobody can control you.'

(Photograph the author)

4

WOMEN OF INDEPENDENCE

'I enjoy independence. I earn my own money. I use my own money. Nobody can control you.' These defiant words of Lee Heng sum up the attitude of the women of the Pearl River Delta and distinguished them from other women in China. Given the traditional opposition to women's emancipation, the degree of independence achieved by the women there was nothing short of miraculous. The key to this extraordinary achievement lay in the women's work practices and unique customs.

In addition to their household duties, it was traditional for the women here to work alongside the men. As this eliminated the necessity of hiring labour, it made the women important contributors to the family income. In the words of Wan Yong Gui: 'The womenfolk helped. Some would help in threshing the stems, some helping to sun the grains. We would help each other. You help me today, I help you tomorrow. In this way, engagement of helpers was avoided.' Her recollection was that women in her village in Tung Koon only worked within it, usually on their own farms. This was not always true of women in other villages or districts. Lee Heng, from San Wui, said that it was common for women in her village to leave it to seek jobs elsewhere. She herself went to work in a sweet shop in Hong Kong when she was sixteen. Lok Ah Kew, from Poon Yue, remembers: 'All the girls in our family worked in my father's fields once they were fourteen and although most women in the village worked in the padi fields, some went to Canton each day to work as domestic servants.' These work practices enabled the women to maintain an economic independence far beyond that of most women in China—the first step towards a life independent of men. Nowhere was this more evident than in the silk-producing region of Shun Tak where girl silk workers were often the main bread-winners of the family. Agnes Smedley observed that awareness of their worth gave them a 'dignified independent bearing'.

Some customs prevalent elsewhere in China were unpopular

in the Pearl River Delta while others were unique to the region. The impact of this increased freedom brought about significant changes, not only to their self-image and attitude generally but also to their life-style.

One of the most significant differences concerned the practice of footbinding. Although this custom was popular throughout most of China, it was hardly practised in the region. Lee Heng confirms: 'There were no women with bound feet in our village.' This underlined their unconventional attitude, and not being crippled meant that they could work properly, and thus were an economic asset to the family. The result was an improved status in the family—much higher than that enjoyed by most other Chinese women. Their position was further enhanced when they remitted money when abroad.

While most Chinese women were restricted to the home and its immediate environs—many travelled no further than one or two kilometres from their houses during their entire lives—the women of the Delta could travel freely. This helps to explain why most female Chinese emigrants came from provinces where footbinding was unpopular, notably Fukien and especially Kwangtung.

Footbinding was not the only factor restricting women to the home; tradition did, too. Women were normally only allowed to leave the home to shop, to attend festivities or funerals, or to visit relatives. In this region, however, there existed unique places—reserved exclusively for girls and women and collectively known as Women's Houses—to which they could freely go. The first was known as a *nui yan uk* (Girls' House). Lau Siew Yong explains: 'A *nui yan uk* was for unmarried girls. It was owned by a widow who would let girls stay free in return for helping her with the housework. They would stay there at night but would go home for their meals. The girls staying there were usually from large families.' Two factors created this situation: the need of the widows for help and companionship, and overcrowding in households. Most dwellings were small and consequently crowded when families were large—sometimes very large. There were fourteen in Lok Ah Kew's family—ten girls, two boys, and her parents. These Girls' Houses thus served the eminently useful purpose of relieving serious congestion in many family homes, and thus enjoyed widespread support.

The girls enjoyed the freedom away from home and the opportunity to meet other girls; the older ones taught younger girls handicraft skills such as sewing and embroidery, and social skills, as well as informing them about religious rites and customs. Thus, denied schooling and the opportunity to otherwise gather freely, the girls were given a unique opportunity at these houses to learn from and to exchange ideas with others. It was a social club, hostel, and school rolled into one. Their experiences here greatly affected their attitudes to life and, especially, marriage. Most amahs had spent some time in a Girls' House.

The other type of place reserved exclusively for females was a variation of the Girls' House. This was the *ku por uk* (Grand-aunts' or Old Maids' House), which usually catered for older unmarried women. In districts such as Shun Tak, *nui yan uk* was the name given to houses for all unmarried females, whether young or old. However, to avoid confusion, the term *ku por uk* will be used in this present work to refer to a house that catered for older unmarried females.

The essential difference between the two was that the girls at a Girls' House were only lodgers while a Grand-aunts' House was owned by the women themselves. In the latter case, the women formed themselves into a co-operative to purchase a house or, more usually, to have one built, or they made individual contributions. According to Choong Hup Yee, 'It cost around one hundred barrels of maize to build a *ku por uk*.' Residency was, therefore, only open to women who had contributed. An exception was sometimes made for an unmarried female relative of one of the group. She would, however, only be allowed to stay for a few days.

There were some variations to this. Occasionally, a doting wealthy father might have such a house built for his daughter who had *sor hei* (taken a vow not to marry). More usually, the house was built by a specific group of unmarried women such as those who had *sor hei* or had been overseas and had returned to retire. In large villages, there were usually several Women's Houses of both types.

The significance of these houses was that it allowed women to live independently of men and with full social acceptance—a rare thing in China.

Marriage customs, when practised, were the same here as elsewhere in China. Ow Ah Tim explains the traditional arrangements:

All marriages were matchmade. The matchmaker would find out the date and time of birth of the man and the woman and consult a fortune-teller or check in the almanac to see if they were suitably matched. If they were suitable, she would continue with the arrangements and would only be paid if it was a successful match.

The matchmaker would go round looking for business and often had a hard time. Sometimes she would be chased away and beaten with a broom.

People with the same surname do not marry. The men would marry women from other villages and bring them back. The only time this does not happen is when there is war like when the Japanese invaded us [the 1937 Sino-Japanese War]. Men then married women in their own villages.

Lau Siew Yong added that the matchmaker would be from the same village or from a neighbouring village. Tong Yuet Ching said that it was normal for all the girls in her village in Chong San to get married. She herself was married when she was twenty-one but without the groom present at the ceremony. She describes her unusual marriage:

The marriage was arranged by a matchmaker from the man's village who knew my mother and his parents. Photos were exchanged and agreement reached after the almanac was consulted. The matchmaker would only be paid if successful. If the family was rich, the marriage was quickly arranged, but if poor, it was very slow; sometimes it took six months to a year to arrange as there was no money for the ceremony and the festivities. I had no choice, but I thought he was handsome. I was not happy to be married because I did not want to leave my village and my husband-to-be was in Singapore.

The marriage ceremony was a simple occasion. It was officiated by his parents in their village. Only close relatives were invited. My parents were paid $21 as a dowry. I was carried to his village in a red sedan chair. As he was not present, his place was taken by a cockerel.

After I was married, I stayed at my parents-in-law's house. Fortunately, they were kind and treated me well. I helped with their farm and they allowed me to visit my own family frequently. My husband remitted money from Singapore for my support and later I travelled there to join him.

Strange as it may seem, it was an accepted custom for a cockerel to be a groom's proxy should he be unable to be present at the wedding ceremony. Hence, marriages could take place when the men were abroad and the women were in China.

Unlike other parts of China, where all marriages were matchmade, there were districts in the Pearl River Delta where this was not the case. Lee Heng said that about half the married women in her San Wui village had their marriages arranged while the other half chose their husbands.

With increased economic independence, there was a marked change in attitude towards the hitherto sacrosanct state of marriage. Many women no longer believed in the inevitability of marriage nor on their dependence on men. The existence of the Women's Houses demonstrated this. These houses were crucial focal points in maintaining attitudes against marriage.

In the Girls' House, the older girls, in particular, inevitably discussed the pros and cons of marriage as they approached marriageable age. They would have been aware of all the problems of being a wife—having to cope with the feared figure of the mother-in-law and to look after all the in-laws, and of losing their independence. It is perhaps not surprising that many did not want to get married after the relative freedom they enjoyed as girls, especially during their stay in a Girls' House. These views on marriage were passed on by the older to the younger girls, thus ensuring their perpetuity

Of the amahs interviewed, more than 80 per cent were not married. Typical reasons which they gave for not wanting to get married included:

I wanted to be independent and didn't want to look after parents-in-law, brothers-in-law, sisters-in-law. (Chan Foon.)

If you marry, you will be controlled by the in-laws and your movements will be restricted. (Ow Ah Tim.)

I was afraid of childbirth and did not want the responsibility of bringing up children. (Chan Ching Lin.)

I was afraid of in-laws. I did not want to be poor like my parents and I liked being independent. (Lau Siew Yong.)

I had heard about unhappy marriages. (Tang Ah Thye.)

I did not want to be a daughter-in-law and I enjoy freedom. (Leong Siew Kee.)

The overall impression they gave was that they valued their independence above all and saw marriage as being an end to that.

Women of the region, it seems, have long been against the tradition of marriage, especially in areas in and around the district of Shun Tak. Some were particularly extreme in their opposition to marriage. In *Things Chinese*, T. C. Lai noted that there was a strange custom in the village of Tai Leong and some other villages in Shun Tak. Nearly all the girls there had a habit of swearing sisterhood to each other, taking vows of celibacy, and looking upon their prospective husbands as enemies. If, as a result of family pressure, they did marry, they would refuse to consummate the marriage, return home on the third day of the wedding, and refuse to return to their husbands. As this refusal meant that they had broken the marriage contract arranged by their parents, they had to pay their husbands to buy a concubine to take their place. Should they be unable to do so, they would commit suicide by taking poison, hanging or drowning, so great was their aversion to marriage.

In some ways, even if exaggerated, these vows are reminiscent of a fanatical version of a schoolgirls' pact and would almost certainly have been taken when they were staying together at a Girls' House. A less extreme version, but no less dramatic, was the ritual performed when any of the girls at a Girls' House got married: a funeral ceremony would be held for her to mourn the loss of her freedom.

Regardless of the importance of economic self-sufficiency, it was, by itself, not enough to enable them to lead independent lives as unmarried women. The concept of 'spinster' or unmarried woman is somewhat alien to traditional Chinese society. Hugh D. R. Baker noted that there was no separate term for it in Chinese, the usual translation being not 'unmarried woman' but 'girl not yet married'—a significant distinction.

Tradition was so strong that despite the refusal to accept marriage as a woman's only viable option, those who did not want to marry but did not want to become nuns had to find a socially acceptable way of remaining unmarried, as the only other unmarried women were prostitutes and concubines. It was the belief that a girl or woman, regardless of age, could not be considered an adult until she was married and that younger brothers and sisters could not marry until she had. Furthermore, only adults could give presents. Finally, as the tradition of ancestor-worship did not cater for unmarried females, it put added pressure on the women to marry.

The apparently insoluble problem of remaining single yet being socially acceptable was resolved by the ingenious custom known as *sor hei*. The literal meaning of *sor hei* is 'comb-up'. The significance of this term lies in the fact that single women usually wore their hair in a plait while married women wore theirs as a bun at the back of the head. Though not always the case, a woman with her hair in a bun usually indicated that she was married.

It was, however, insufficient merely to comb her hair into a bun. It was necessary to perform it with the appropriate vows at a proper ceremony, i.e. for it to be ritualized. The ceremony itself was quite simple and could take place at a temple, an ancestral hall, or even at home, before the altar. In all cases, the crucial vows made before the altar were the vows not to marry and to lead a life of celibacy. Most women took their vows in China before they emigrated, but they could also be taken abroad.

In effect, the *sor hei* ceremony was equivalent to that of marriage. It was preferable that the parents and elder brothers gave their permission, but if this was not forthcoming, the ceremony could still proceed. As in marriage, a fortune-teller or almanac would be consulted to determine the most propitious day to hold the ceremony. New clothes would be made for the occasion and a feast held after it.

The other main difference to a conventional marriage was that only female friends and relatives would normally be invited to the ceremony and the girl's parents would not be present. Friends of the girl would give her a *hong pau*—a red packet containing money—while her relatives would give the 'red packet' to her parents. Wan Yong Gui describes the *sor hei* ceremony in her village in Tung Koon:

Choose an auspicious day. A suit of new clothes, like for a wedding. Blue, black or grey were our choice. Get a priest to perform the prayers with offerings of wine, vegetarian foods, rice and fruits.

The preparation for the ceremony was usually done with the help of an old woman or a widow with no children. They would make all the necessary arrangements. They knew what to do. You just made a new dress and they helped with the rest. They were not professionals but odd-jobbers and were rewarded with a *hong pau*.

Anyone taking the vow would change into new clothes and have her hair combed into a bun at the back of the head and secured with a large pin, with the help of the odd-jobber. She would then take her vow with the help of the priest. Pray to the God of Heaven. Pray to Kwan Yin. There was no need to powder your face. Only brides needed to make up. A bun represented [the status of being] grown-up and no more a child—just like marriage meant [that one was] grown-up.

If one was rich, then there would be a feast, just like a wedding. It would be held the next day. Relatives, friends and other vow-takers were all invited.

14   Detail of hair worn in a bun.
A bun usually indicated that the woman was married or,
in the case of the amahs, such as this one, was *sor hei*,
i.e. had taken vows of celibacy.
(Courtesy Joanna Wormald)

Leong Ah Pat adds that, in her village in Nam Hoi, there was also a concluding ceremony at the parents' house:

At the house, there would be a lantern and two pails of water. The lantern would be lit and it would be carried into the house with the two buckets on a pole on the shoulder. The lantern would be placed beside the altar and the water poured into the water jar. The water signified long life and good health for the family and the lantern signified a bright light to shine on everyone, i.e. a prosperous and good life.

A tea ceremony would then be performed and the tea would be served to the parents who would not have attended the *sor hei* ceremony. Guests then would be invited for lunch or dinner.

Chan Foon and Ow Ah Tim, however, maintained that in Shun Tak, the carrying of the lantern and water across the threshold was only done by second wives or concubines. To further complicate matters, once a woman was *sor hei*, she could choose whether to wear her hair in a bun or in a plait once again. Most would usually wear it in a bun.

Usually the reasons given for wanting to be *sor hei* were synonymous with those given for not wanting to get married. There were some, however, who also wanted to take their vows in order to free themselves from the restrictions of their own families—an important factor in their desire for independence. Wan Yong Gui explains, 'Once you are *sor hei*, you can keep whatever money you earn; it's up to you to keep or give. Your father can't control you, neither can your mother. There was no further responsibility to your family—as if you were married.' This was a reaction against the First Obeying which gave fathers total control over their daughters, including the right to any money earned. For many women, therefore, independence meant being free from the restrictions of marriage as well as those of the home.

The main problem facing *sor hei* women was that they could no longer live at home, just as they could not have done so had they married. While some compassionate fathers might allow them to stay at home, tradition decreed that they could not die there. Thus, once married or *sor hei*, they neither belonged to their family nor could they live with them. Consequently, the Women's Houses were essential to them in life as well as in death, and of particular importance to emigrant *sor hei* women who needed somewhere to live on their intended return to China.

Sor hei vows were sometimes taken abroad. Those who took them abroad rather than in China usually did so because they or their families could not afford the cost of the feast. Many women

15   Leong Hock Kam
A gentle lady and still independent in spirit at eighty-two.
(Photograph the author)

who were single when they emigrated did not bother to take their *sor hei* vows abroad as the social conditions which made their vows in China necessary were no longer relevant. Although there were some amahs who were married, most were single and a sizeable proportion of them were *sor hei*. The ceremony could also be performed posthumously by relatives or friends of the deceased to ensure that she could be worshipped after death.

This unique practice was a feature of the customs pertaining to women of the Pearl River Delta. Together with their ability to earn a living, it freed them from the restrictions of both marriage and the home, and allowed them to lead independent lives. This independence enabled the women of the region to be foremost among all Chinese female emigrants. Given the hardships suffered in China, it seems surprising that they did not emigrate in any numbers until the second half of the nineteenth century—in fact, no Chinese women did. But then, emigration from China was forbidden.

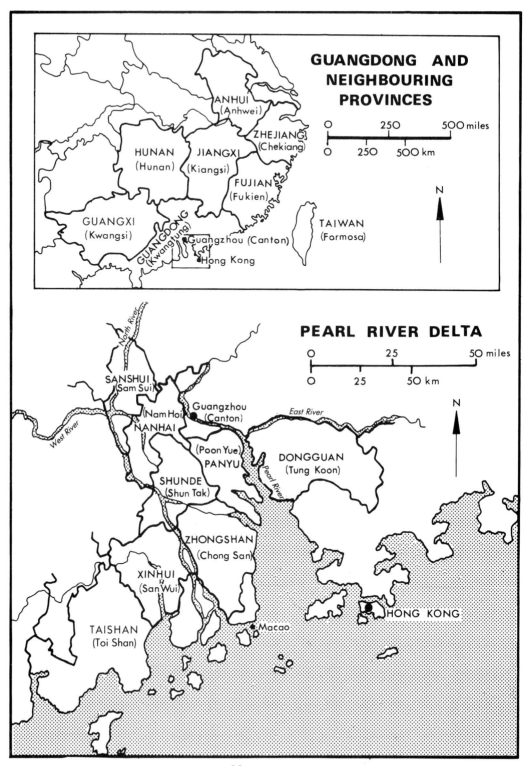

GUANGDONG AND NEIGHBOURING PROVINCES

ANHUI (Anhwei)

ZHEJIANG (Chekiang)

HUNAN (Hunan)

JIANGXI (Kiangsi)

FUJIAN (Fukien)

GUANGXI (Kwangsi)

GUANGDONG (Kwangtung)

Guangzhou (Canton)

Hong Kong

TAIWAN (Formosa)

0   250   500 miles
0   250   500 km

N

PEARL RIVER DELTA

0   25   50 miles
0   25   50 km

N

North River

SANSHUI (Sam Sui)

West River

(Nam Hoi)

NANHAI

Guangzhou (Canton)

East River

(Poon Yue)

PANYU

DONGGUAN (Tung Koon)

SHUNDE (Shun Tak)

Pearl River

ZHONGSHAN (Chong San)

XINHUI (San Wui)

TAISHAN (Toi Shan)

Macao

HONG KONG

Map 2

5

ENTERPRISING SOJOURNERS

EMIGRATION from China was legally forbidden, on pain of death by decapitation. The Manchus, in particular, were opposed to it, in the belief that it was an unfilial act for any Chinese citizen to desert his homeland for another country. Another reason, a more pragmatic one, was that being highly unpopular, they suspected that all emigrants would be plotting the Dynasty's downfall. This law was theoretically in operation until 1860, when the foreign powers forced China to discard it; but it was not until 1894 that it was formally repealed.

In practice, however, this law was not strictly enforced—at least, where the men were concerned—and several million, mostly from Kwangtung and Fukien, managed to 'remove to foreign islands'.

Port officials turned a blind eye to the emigration of the men as long as the women did not leave. They reasoned that married men would have to return to visit wives and families, and single men would return with savings to marry local women, thereby providing them with the opportunity of obtaining 'squeeze' money from the returning emigrants. They were also able to take a percentage of the remittances sent by the men abroad for the support of families left behind. As their departure was illegal, the emigrants were in no position to argue.

Furthermore, damaging conflicts, both internal and external, left the government in too weak a position to enforce the law effectively, even if it had wanted to. Lastly, the Manchus were confident of the men's return as the ancient tradition of ancestor-worship made it important for them to be buried with their ancestors. While most races regarded emigration as permanent, the Chinese did not. They saw it only as a temporary measure—a sojourn—always intending to return to China once they had made their fortunes. Although this objective was often not realized and

16   Canton junk, 1873.
Ships like this one were widely used in the early migration of the Chinese.
(Courtesy Wellcome Institute Library, London)

many were forced to stay abroad, it remained the desire of every Chinese emigrant to return home one day, dead or alive. The case of Hoo Ah Kay, more popularly known as Whampoa, a highly successful and well-known Cantonese businessman in Singapore, exemplified this. Despite his 'Englishness' and full acceptance by Singapore's colonial society, he expressed a wish to be buried in China. Consequently, after his death in 1880 at the age of sixty-four, his remains were taken back to China and buried on Danes Island, opposite Canton.

Most Chinese emigrated due to the extreme hardships suffered in China and to the lack of prospects. Foremost among natural disasters were flood, drought, and famine. The provinces of Fukien and Kwangtung, however, were luckier than most and there were few records of such catastrophes. Nevertheless, in the latter part of the seventeenth century, an Imperial edict recorded that annual floods and droughts had 'left the people exhausted'. This led to the first sizeable emigration to the Nanyang as well as to neighbouring provinces and Formosa (Taiwan). More recently, in the *1921 Census of British Malaya*, it was noted that in the period 1918-20, there was a sharp increase of immigrants to Singapore, particularly females, 'due no doubt to famine and unsettled conditions in South China'. Similarly, China was stricken by drought in 1929 and by floods in 1931.

The Manchus were widely disliked for their oppressive, reactionary, and corrupt rule. An example of their style of government was their ruthless execution of the Imperial system of punishment. The penalty for highway robbery was crucifixion or decapitation. Treasonable offences resulted in the guilty party being whittled away, a joint at a time, until his body was sliced into pieces by the executioner. And anyone caught housebreaking or stealing was forced to stand in front of the house or store he had violated for a specified period, during which all his bodily functions had to be performed while imprisoned in a device known as a cangue.

Spirited local opposition, particularly in Fukien and Kwangtung, caused the Manchus considerable headaches. One particular thorn in their side was a fervently anti-Manchu pirate known as Koxinga. Operating from Formosa in the mid-seventeenth century, he regularly raided the mainland. His operations angered the Manchus so greatly that when they discovered he was replenishing his supplies in Fukien, they evacuated the people along the coasts of Fukien, Chekiang, and Kwangtung and

17 Man in cangue, *c*.1874.
This was the punishment for housebreaking or theft still in operation
during the early part of the twentieth century.
(Courtesy Wellcome Institute Library, London)

18 West River floods, Canton, July 1915.
Floods such as these were regular occurrences in the Pearl River Delta.
(Courtesy Hong Kong Government)

R FLOODS
JLY 1915

destroyed the villages, livestock, and crops in those areas. Savage treatment like this did not endear the Manchus to the rest of the population. The culmination of internal opposition to their rule was the massively destructive Taiping Rebellion of 1850–64, which not only killed millions but also badly damaged the land and destroyed whole farming communities, resulting in considerable migration within China to fertile provinces such as Kwangtung, and swelling an already dense population. This added pressure caused many to leave.

However, even though conditions were such that many sought to emigrate, it would still not have been possible unless there were suitable countries to which to go. 'Suitable' in this context means countries which either welcomed immigrants or, at least, would not object to their entry. From the point of view of would-be emigrants, these should be countries offering good prospects and preferably ones with which they are familiar. Few voluntarily go to unfamiliar countries.

For many centuries, China considered itself the Middle Kingdom—the land between Heaven and Earth—and superior to all others. There was thus no need to associate or to trade with others. Marco Polo's tales of the splendours and wealth of China whetted the appetites of thirteenth-century Europe. But it was not until three centuries later that any European nation managed to establish trade links with China. The Portuguese were the first to do so, with a base in Macao in 1516. The Spanish were next, using Manila in the Philippines as their base. From 1730 to 1842, they were the only foreigners allowed to use the port of Amoy (Xiamen). Not until 1762 were the Dutch able to maintain an interest at Canton. The English were fairly early starters in their first attempts to trade in 1596 but were unable to set up a base until 1670, also in Canton.

Despite general opposition to foreign trade, the Manchus had a temporary change of heart in 1685. An Imperial Decree declared all ports open to foreign trade. Canton and Amoy, however, continued to maintain their status as the premier entrepôts. A further edict in 1757, however, allowed only Canton to be open to foreigners. This trade, however sporadic, provided the people in and around the ports of Macao, Swatow (Shantou) in East Kwangtung, and especially Amoy and Canton, with the opportunity of coming into contact with foreigners.

Ships brought news of activities of distant countries such as North America, Australia, and New Zealand, as well as neighbouring countries in the Nanyang. News of the discovery of gold in 1848 in California, a few years later in Victoria, Australia, and in the early 1860s in Otago, New Zealand, attracted tens of thousands of men. They were also recruited in large numbers in the second half of the nineteenth century to work in the mines and on the railroads of North America. In *Your Chinese Roots*, Thomas Tsu-wee Tan describes their efforts on the building of some of the American railroads as one of the mightiest feats of Chinese labour. Most of the Chinese, however, went to countries closer to home—Hong Kong, Singapore, and Malaya mainly but also to Thailand, Indonesia, and the Philippines.

However, of all the early Western nations trading with China, only Britain was interested in establishing permanent settlements in the Far East. Although the Portuguese were first on the scene, they were neither keen on establishing such settlements nor in trying to attract settlers. They saw their role primarily as crusaders and, due to their violent methods of conversion, were hated in all the countries around Malaya. The high cost of trading in Melaka, their first settlement, also caused many Chinese junks to divert to Patani in Thailand. The Dutch took Melaka from the Portuguese in 1641 but did little to improve the situation. Although appreciating the need to attract the hard-working Chinese to develop the colony, the Dutch East India Company did little to implement it.

In the end, only the British set out to attract the Chinese, knowing that these indefatigable workers would help to enrich their new territories. They started soon after establishing Penang as a colony in 1786 and capturing Melaka from the Dutch in 1795. Victor Purcell, in *The Chinese in Malaya*, noted that Sir Francis Light, first Governor of Penang, regarded the Chinese as 'the most valuable part' of the inhabitants. 'Valuable' here, however, could have had another meaning other than 'useful'. Taxes derived from the men's fondness for opium and gambling provided a lucrative source of revenue.

At that time, Britain was also the only nation attempting to treat Chinese emigrants well. They had a horrendous time in the goldfields of America, Australia, and New Zealand, frequently being victims of vicious racist attacks. By contrast, the British, though often ignorant of Chinese customs, established a Charter of Justice in 1807 in Penang. Its aims were to ensure the religious and cultural freedom of all immigrants and helped to attract the Chinese to Penang.

19   Beach Street, Penang, c.1900.

Penang was the first British settlement in the
Malay Peninsula, colonized in 1786.
(Courtesy Museum Department, Malaysia)

Singapore, founded by Sir Stamford Raffles in 1819, proved to be an even greater success. It grew astronomically from a reputed 150 inhabitants (120 Malays and 30 Chinese) in February 1819 to an estimated 5,000, mainly Chinese, within a few months. This estimate by Raffles himself was probably somewhat optimistic. A more realistic figure was that assessed in 1823 of just over 10,500 with the Chinese component being around 3,300, or just under a third. These early settlers came mainly from Melaka and the Riau Archipelago, attracted by excellent trading and agricultural prospects as well as by the reputation of the British. Later immigrants came from China itself—chiefly the Hokkiens, the Cantonese, and the Teochews, and smaller groups such as the Hakkas and the Hainanese. Eventually, they comprised approximately three-quarters of the total population in 1901. This proportion established by the census figures of the 1901 Straits Settlements [Singapore, Melaka, and Penang] Blue Book has remained almost constant ever since.

In nineteenth-century Malaya, the rapidly developing industries of tin and crops such as rubber, pepper, and gambier created so great a demand for the 'industrious Chinese' that the British, through their Chinese agents, often resorted to unscrupulous methods of obtaining Chinese labour. The organized importation of Chinese labour for the plantations and mines—the coolie trade—became known as the 'pig business' due to the similarity to the buying and selling of pigs; and the men so obtained were known as 'piglings'. With the hardships in China, it was not difficult for agents to lure many men over with tales of the easy money to be made and the offer of a free passage. Alternatively, they were enticed to towns such as Amoy and Canton and brought to gambling-houses designed to relieve them of their money and to put them seriously in debt. In order to repay those debts, settled by the agents, the men had no choice but to emigrate. Another method of obtaining cheap labour was by the 'credit-ticket' system, whereby the emigrant had his fare paid in return for working without pay for a number of years. The British effort to recruit Chinese labour proved so successful that it created an almost totally male Chinese population in their settlements with all the inherent social problems of such an imbalanced situation.

Hong Kong, with an almost totally Chinese population, was a different situation. With most of its inhabitants being Cantonese from the Pearl River Delta, there has always been a steady traffic between Kwangtung and Hong Kong. Thus it was never necessary to attract the Chinese there. Nevertheless, due to the traditional pattern of emigration, the population in nineteenth-century Hong Kong was also predominantly male.

A point worth noting in the context of Chinese emigration is that, outside the Far East, the Chinese mainly emigrated to English-speaking countries such as North America, Australia, and New Zealand—a result of early trade links, the reputation of the British, and of course, the discovery of gold. In Britain, the early Chinese settlers were seamen who jumped ship at the main ports of London and Liverpool in the early 1870s, after the Suez Canal was opened; this explains why the early Chinese immigrants in Britain were concentrated around the dock areas of those two cities. However, compared with the Chinese population of the Far East, the number of Chinese in all these countries is small. It should not be forgotten, however, that unlike the British settlements in the Far East, these countries did not set out to attract Chinese emigrants. In fact, their presence was barely tolerated and, until quite recently, they were subjected to considerable racial discrimination. It is perhaps also worth remembering that despite their early contact with the Chinese, there were and are no large numbers of Chinese in any settlement or country established by the early trading nations such as Portugal, Spain or Holland, outside the Far East.

One curious factor about Chinese emigration is although the north suffered more natural hardships than the south, as well as being less fertile, northerners did not leave in large numbers. Two acres (1 acre = 0.405 hectare) could support a family of five in the south while five acres were needed in the north.

Other factors which are important to the emigration process are access to ports and contact with foreigners. By this reasoning, the people of Chekiang and Kiangsu should therefore have been among the main emigrants. Both provinces have important entrepôts—Ningpo (Ningbo) in Chekiang and Shanghai in Kiangsu—providing access abroad and contact with the West. Shanghai, in fact, was once considered the most important of all the Treaty ports. But here, too, the people left only in comparatively small numbers.

Proximity and similarity of climate are also given to explain why some people choose to emigrate to certain countries. The natives of Kwangsi (Guangxi) in the south thus ought to have contributed a large number of emigrants as that province is

20 The interior of Kwangtung.

This 1870 photograph shows the mountains that separated
much of Kwangtung from the rest of China.
(Courtesy Wellcome Institute Library, London)

closest to countries in the Nanyang and has a similar climate; yet they only formed a small part of those who left.

The vast majority of Chinese emigrants came from two provinces in the south: predominantly the Hokkiens from Fukien and the Teochews and Cantonese from Kwangtung. The Hokkiens and Teochews, however, emigrated only to countries in South-East Asia; the Cantonese were not only present in large numbers in Singapore and Malaya but virtually made up all those who emigrated to countries away from the Far East. A brief examination of the two provinces may provide an explanation for this.

Much of Fukien and Kwangtung is separated from the rest of China by vast mountain ranges, which created a social as well as physical barrier. Being more isolated, the people here were less influenced by events and trends elsewhere and developed greater independence—explaining, perhaps, why footbinding, widespread elsewhere in China, was unpopular here.

Due to physical conditions of the region, the natives of the Pearl River Delta in south-eastern Kwangtung became especially resourceful. People here have long had to earn their living in ways other than farming. The mountainous, less arable parts like Toi Shan (Taishan), for example, were unable to sustain their inhabitants for more than four months of the year. (As a matter of interest, the predominant Chinese population of North America, Canada, Australia, and New Zealand all originated from Toi Shan.) The network of waterways not only served the needs of the people in terms of irrigation and fishing but made access to ports like Canton and Hong Kong simple. With the opportunities available there, trading became a popular occupation and much valuable experience was gained in all aspects of business—buying, selling, and financing.

Notwithstanding the diverse causes of emigration and the factors which affect it, there are certain qualities which every potential emigrant must possess if he wishes to survive satisfactorily abroad. In attempting to explain why most Chinese emigrants came from Fukien and Kwangtung, writers like Chen Ta finally reasoned that the people there possessed certain cultural traits lacking in the rest of the population which 'predispose them for foreign adventure'. Purcell had a similar view, concluding that their 'superior enterprise' was the most important factor. He even thought that it was probably more important than all the other reasons put together.

Once established, emigration became self-perpetuating. Regular contact between inhabitants and returning emigrants ensured continuation of the process. This was especially true of countries in the Nanyang—a fact confirmed by all the amahs interviewed. They emigrated to countries like Singapore, Malaya, or Hong Kong simply because they already knew someone there or had heard about those countries from someone who had been there.

Thus, until the middle of the nineteenth century, emigration from China was an entirely male affair and illegal. But once the Manchus started losing their power, they found it impossible to maintain their 'closed door policy'. The tide began turning from the time of the Taiping Rebellion when the chaotic conditions made it increasingly difficult for them to maintain their grip. For the first time, it was possible for Chinese women to leave. Once the law forbidding emigration was discarded in 1860, there was a flood of people leaving, men as well as women. Like the men, the women came from Fukien and Kwangtung and they too possessed the essential ingredient of 'superior enterprise'.

An article in the *Singapore Free Press* on 12 December 1841 noted that it was believed there was not 'any Chinese woman proper' on the island. The description 'Chinese woman proper' refers to the fact that women who were usually referred to as 'Chinese' were of mixed descent, i.e. descendants of the offspring of Chinese men and Malay women, known locally as Baba Chinese or simply Babas. They were also known as Peranakan or Straits Chinese.

While men were 'allowed' to emigrate, the law against female emigration was strictly enforced. The article mentioned above demonstrated the effectiveness of that control. The reasons why the Chinese officials only permitted male emigration are well known. What perhaps is less well understood is why the men themselves did not want their women to leave.

By far the most important reason was that of ancestor-worship. This ancient custom made it essential for rites to be maintained. Although attendance at ancestral halls, where the tablets of the dead were kept, was a male privilege, women were allowed to perform those rites if, for any reason, the men were absent. Thus, it was necessary for the women to remain when their menfolk were abroad. Another reason was filial piety. It was the duty of sons to look after their parents; but in their absence, it became the wives' responsibility. Hence filial piety demanded that the wives remain in their husbands' absence.

Social custom further decreed that women should remain at

21 River settlement, c.1900.

The network of waterways provided the people of the Pearl River Delta
with a ready means of travel as well as access to ports.
(Courtesy Lim Kheng Chye)

home. The Hainanese, in particular, were opposed to the emigration of their women and none were allowed to leave the island
of Hainan, off the southern tip of Kwangtung Province, till 1924.
The *1921 Census of British Malaya* noted that the Hailam
(Hainanese) custom which forbade them to bring their women to
the country was well known and rigidly followed but could offer
no satisfactory explanation. This attitude was amply demonstrated in an earlier episode in 1910 recorded by Song Ong Siang
in his *One Hundred Years' History of the Chinese in Singapore*. A
Hailam woman had allegedly arrived in Singapore and was staying at a house in Middle Road. Some 2,000 Hailam houseboys and
shopkeepers stormed the house in order to apprehend the woman
over this apparent breach of their customs. It turned out to be a
false alarm as no such woman was found.

The Chinese also felt that children should be brought up in
China and that sons, even if born to non-Chinese wives abroad,
should be educated there. It was, therefore, the responsibility of
the women, whether wives or other female family members, to
look after them.

A more practical reason were the severe conditions abroad. In
the early years, conditions were harsh and the mortality rate high,
and thus considered unsuitable for women. Furthermore, as most
emigrants were poor, there was no point in bringing a wife whom
they would not be able to support. There was also no particular
attraction for women, whether single or married, to emigrate.
Single men who succeeded either went back to China to marry or
remained to wed a local girl, while the successful married ones
returned to settle.

In the early years of female emigration, there were few single
'respectable' women. The majority of single women arriving in
the Nanyang in the nineteenth century were directly or indirectly
connected with prostitution. Prior to 1870, almost all the single
women arriving had been specifically imported by the secret
societies for financial gain and as a means of extending their
sphere of influence. This practice continued well into the twentieth century until the importation of prostitutes was officially
banned.

In terms of the early emigration of women, Hong Kong was
easily the most important destination. Formerly part of China, it
has been inhabited by the Cantonese since the fifteenth century.
Hong Kong was ceded to Britain in 1842 after the Opium War
and has since become the main home of the Cantonese outside

China. About 98 per cent of the population are Chinese, with the Cantonese predominant. After 1842, it quickly surpassed Macao in terms of importance as a port. There has thus long been a two-way contact between Hong Kong and Canton, as a consequence of which the pattern of immigration here is markedly different from that of other countries. The natives of the Pearl River Delta did not view Hong Kong as another country and thus did not consider going there as 'emigration'. None the less, it was another country, and the most important one for both men and women from Kwangtung. It was also the stepping-stone to the Nanyang for virtually all Cantonese women. They were, however, not the first Chinese women to arrive in Singapore. That distinction belongs to the Hokkien women from Amoy.

Lim Joo Hock, in his academic exercise, 'Chinese Female Immigration into the Straits Settlements 1860–1901', maintained that it was probably true that there was no female immigration into Singapore until the year 1853. The significance of that year is revealed by C. B. Buckley in *An Anecdotal History of Old Times in Singapore 1819–1867*, in which he reported the arrival of many Chinese vessels from Amoy in the latter part of 1853 as a result of a disturbance there.

The 'disturbance' referred to was the Amoy Rebellion of May 1853. This was a local insurrection against the Manchus started by one Un Wee, after Tan Keng Chin, a Hokkien who had acquired the status of a British subject in Singapore, was killed. Tan had organized an off-shoot of the Triads called the Small Knife Society in Amoy around 1848-9. This group had planned the Amoy coup as well as a later one at Shanghai in September. He was working as a clerk—some say a compradore—for Jardine's (a leading mercantile firm) when he was tortured to death by the local *taotai* (provincial officials). His successor, Un Wee, swore vengeance and engineered the rising of 1853. Though successful, it was short-lived. Successful, because the Manchus were unpopular and there was considerable local support for the rebels, but short-lived due to poor organization and leadership.

Among others, the ships brought the wives and families of Amoy merchants trading in Singapore who had been sending supplies and financial support to the rebels there. When the rebellion was crushed, the merchants, fearing reprisals against their families in Amoy, had them evacuated.

Buckley also mentioned that it was hoped that the arrival of the wives and families would have a 'beneficial influence' on the

Chinese section of the population. This last reference revealed the urgency of the social situation in the British colony, where the female to male ratio was 1:8, with few of the women being Chinese. It also echoed British concern as the almost entirely male world of the Chinese made them unruly and difficult to handle.

The arrival of Chinese females in Singapore in 1853 did not pass unnoticed by the Chinese secret societies. They were quick to recognize the financial advantages of having women under their control. Their ambition of importing women from China for immoral purposes was unwittingly helped by the desperate desire of the British to increase the Chinese female population— although, undoubtedly, this was not what the authorities had in mind. The lax immigration controls allowed many such women to enter.

Although prostitution was not approved, the bans on brothels and the importation of prostitutes did not become official until well into the twentieth century. One reason for this was the difficulty of enforcement due to the control the traffickers had over their victims—a combination of fear and filial piety. Many girls who had been sold by their parents to the traffickers were so conditioned by tradition concerning their obligations to their 'buyers' that they regarded their 'buyers' as having parental authority over them.

Another difficulty involved distinguishing genuine female immigrants from those brought in as prostitutes. The women entering for prostitution usually claimed to be widows or to be joining their husbands; if they were girls, the assertion would be made that they were daughters of the women bringing them in. These deceptions were easy to maintain as few British officials understood Chinese.

The seriousness of the situation was eventually acknowledged by the authorities when they appointed Henry Pickering, literate in Chinese and fluent in several dialects, as Protector of Chinese in 1877 to look after the interests of the Chinese in Singapore. In 1880, a Protector of Chinese was appointed for Penang and eventually Protectorates were established throughout Malaya.

Pickering's job was to concentrate on stopping the abuses connected with the importation of labour. It also included tackling the secret societies as well as dealing with the problems of prostitution and female exploitation generally. Despite his knowledge of the Chinese, his ability and enthusiasm, as well as the respect in which he was held, the problems of female exploitation continued for many years. Importation of prostitutes was not banned until 1927 and brothels not made illegal till 1930, some fifty years after his appointment. The other major concern, the exploitation of girls imported as *mui tsai*, was not dealt with until 1937.

The first sizeable emigration of Cantonese women occurred as a result of the Taiping Rebellion. With many of their men already in the Nanyang and the goldfields of North America and elsewhere, it was left to the women to support the family. But with few prospects of work, they were eventually left with no other choice than to consider emigration. Unlike the Hokkien women, many of whom were joining husbands in the Nanyang, few Cantonese were so fortunate. With tradition insisting that women married to men abroad stay at home to look after parents-in-law and to rear children, it was left to the single women to emigrate. Fortunately, they were able-bodied (i.e. did not have bound feet), were independent by Chinese standards, and shared the same spirit of enterprise as their menfolk.

Most were deliberately enticed there by agents sent by the secret societies to recruit them. With the desperate conditions prevailing, it was not difficult for agents, who usually came from the same district as the women themselves, to convince them that going abroad was their only chance of survival and the best means of helping their families. The women were told of the good living to be made as domestic servants or seamstresses and that it was easy to land rich merchants as husbands. Should they already be married, promises would be made to reunite them with their husbands. The lure proved irresistible and many women emigrated as a result.

The demand for females was so great that solitary young girls were simply kidnapped and sold either as *mui tsai* or as 'sing-song girls' for brothels. Another source of supply were orphanages, where procuresses would 'adopt' young girls. There was, of course, the tradition of daughters being sold in times of hardship. The trade was centred principally around Canton, from where the girls were sent to Hong Kong. Those not destined for Hong Kong were forcibly detained, pending arrangements to take them to Singapore and other parts of the Nanyang.

This was the sordid business that Henry Pickering later tried unsuccessfully to deal with. It was estimated by the Legislative Council in Singapore in 1899, that 80 per cent of the inmates of brothels had been deceived into the life by traffickers. These abuses continued even after their arrival. Being penniless, they had their fares paid for them. In exchange, they had to sign an acknowledgement or agreement of servitude which 'bound them to their keepers' until their debts were discharged. This was similar to the credit-ticket system used for the men. In both cases, they were often treated little better than slaves. The women fared worse, not only in having to work as prostitutes but also in being restricted to the premises by brothel-keepers who employed *samseng* (hooligans) to control them.

It was a widespread problem. Cantonese women were employed as prostitutes throughout the Nanyang. Laura Jackson noted in *Chinese Women in South-East Asia* that Cantonese women must have formed a large proportion of the prostitutes in Siam (Thailand) as well as in Malaya. Until 1930, many Cantonese women were directly or indirectly involved with prostitution. This gave them an unjustified, though perhaps understandable, reputation of being women of 'easy virtue'.

In Singapore, as elsewhere in Malaya, efforts were made to safeguard girls and young women arriving from China as well as *mui tsai* who had been badly treated. The Society for the Protection of Women and Children, known as the Po Leung Kuk, was formed in 1885. Run by a committee of prominent Chinese, presided over by the Secretary of Chinese Affairs with the local Protector of Chinese as his deputy, its specific purpose was to protect the girls and women from exploitation and abuse.

Its physical reality was the establishment of an institution or home in which girls could be brought up and educated to prepare them for marriage to 'respectable Chinese'. It therefore took over the traditional parental role of preparing daughters for marriage. With the general shortage of Chinese women, the demand for brides was considerable. A man who wanted a bride had first to make an application to the home. If considered suitable, he would be interviewed to determine his job, character, and economic status, among other details, and if satisfactory could he only then obtain a bride. Over the years, the Po Leung Kuk provided many Chinese men with brides. After its formation, all females entering Singapore or Malaya were interviewed by the authorities, including an officer from the Chinese Protectorate.

The situation was considerably worse in Hong Kong, where the emigration of women from Kwangtung on a large scale followed the same basic pattern as that of Singapore and Malaya—

arrival of women as prostitutes and *mui tsai*. It was noted that in 1844, two years after Hong Kong was ceded to the British, there were more than 13,000 residents in the city of Victoria but only just over 300 families; and of about 400 permanent brick houses occupied by the Chinese, only 13 were private dwellings, the rest apparently being houses of 'ill-repute'. This pattern carried on unchecked. In 1876, there were around 25,000 women and 81,000 men, and if a local Chinese doctor's estimate in 1877 that only 25 per cent of the women were 'respectable' can be relied on, it meant that at least 18,000 women were involved in prostitution.

The problem of the *mui tsai* was harder to resolve in Hong Kong than in the Nanyang, as the practice was widely accepted. Many of the most influential Chinese businessmen in Hong Kong who supported the *mui tsai* system formed the Po Leung Kuk in 1878, similar to those set up in Singapore and Malaya. Its main function, however, was to apprehend the kidnappers, a consequence of which was that many women and girls landed into the hands of the society which then had to care for them till they were repatriated to their homes or, if adult and willing, married off. Children who were unclaimed or whose families could not be contacted were put up for adoption. Repatriation, being impractical, did not occur in Singapore or Malaya.

The bans on the importation of prostitutes and on brothels in 1927 and 1930 respectively changed the nature of female immigration to Singapore and Malaya. Previously it had been relatively easy for women and girls to enter, but once the bans took effect, entry was more difficult. All unattached females entering thereafter had to have a bona fide sponsor or proof of employment, or both. Hong Kong was unaffected as there were no immigration restrictions placed on the entry of either men or women from China. But the events which drastically altered the pattern of female emigration from China were the Depression of the 1920s and the collapse of the silk industry in the 1930s. They brought about the departure of thousands of Cantonese women from the Pearl River Delta in the 1930s.

22 Arrival of Cantonese women in Singapore in the 1930s.

Barefoot and hopeful—a new life and the start of the era
of the Cantonese amah in the Far East.

(Photographer unknown)

6

DUTIFUL DAUGHTERS

THE arrival of the Cantonese women in the 1930s in search of work, marked a significant change in their development as independent women. Although all of them had been important contributors to the family income, most had worked within the home environment or close to it. Thus, they were still bound by prevailing social conventions. But once they emigrated, they were able to lead lives of unprecedented independence and freedom—not only from men, but also from the restrictions of family and their home environment. They were, however, still not free of family ties and their emigration was as much a demonstration of their filial piety as it was of their independence. Most of the emigrant women were single. Filial responsibility was so strong that unmarried daughters would feel duty-bound to support their parents in times of need. It could even extend to daughters who had been sold.

The Depression caused considerable unemployment in Malaya and Singapore and thousands of men were repatriated to China at a cost of several million dollars, it being considered cheaper than having to provide relief in the long term. A great many Cantonese were affected—in the rubber and, especially, the tin industries of Malaya, where they formed a substantial part of the work-force, and in Singapore, where they were much involved in construction. Repatriation was voluntary and many thousands took advantage of the offer. In August 1930, the Immigration Restriction Ordinance came into effect, limiting male immigration.

Until 1929, there were no immigration restrictions in Malaya and Singapore but the Ordinance, thereafter, specifically controlled the entry of men. In 1929, the last year of unrestricted entry, the number of Chinese male immigrants was just over 195,000; in 1930, 151,000; and in 1931, when the Ordinance took effect, it plunged to just under 50,000. It was later replaced by the more comprehensive Aliens Ordinance in 1933, the stated object of which was the regulation of the admission of aliens 'in accordance with the political, social and economic needs of Malaya'. This introduced, in effect, a quota system based on the selection of suitable immigrants on a qualitative basis. This severe reduction created stiff competition among potential immigrants and greatly increased the cost of passages for new male immigrants, known as *sinkheh*. The new Ordinance further reduced the number to 1,000 a month, i.e. 12,000 a year or only about 6 per cent of the 1929 figure. But even with a quota of 12,000 men, it was still substantially more than the total of around 5,000 admitted into the United States during the entire decade from 1931 to 1940.

Repatriation of the men meant that families in China dependent on remittances from abroad no longer had these vital means of support. The situation was exacerbated by widespread food shortages following destructive floods. The crucial final blow was the decline of the silk industry caused by the development of artificial silk or rayon and most severely felt in the Shun Tak region, a major silk-producing area. But fortunately, although limiting the entry of men, the Immigration Ordinance placed no restrictions on women until 1938, when a monthly quota of 500 was introduced. Consequently, a considerable number of Cantonese women arrived in place of the men. It was estimated that there was a migrational gain of 190,000 women from the Pearl River Delta, mainly from the Shun Tak and Tung Koon districts, between 1933 and 1938. Once employed, the women regularly sent funds home. Family dependence on these remittances improved the women's status even further. For the first time, daughters were even able to have a say in how the family income should be spent.

The situation in Hong Kong was different. There was no repatriation. Neither were there any immigration restrictions. It was not until 1949 that Hong Kong first exercised legal control over 'people of Chinese race'. Furthermore, the intrinsic ties between Hong Kong and Kwangtung Province were demonstrated in 1950, when, because of the massive increase in population following the Communist Revolution of 1949, entry permits were required by all Chinese coming from China—except for the natives of Kwangtung. Nevertheless, Hong Kong was as badly affected by the Depression as elsewhere and jobs were equally scarce. It was also not the prosperous city of the 1980s and unable to offer the employment opportunities available in the Nanyang—even when conditions began improving in the latter part of the 1930s.

Unlike most female emigration in the past, these women left voluntarily—that is, they had not been duped into leaving—and most were single. This influx of women did much to restore the sex ratio and alleviate some of the earlier social problems created by the imbalance. In fact, the combination of male repatriation and female immigration led to an unprecedented excess of Cantonese females. The *1931 Census of British Malaya* recorded about 6 Cantonese females to every 10 males but by the next Census in 1947, the proportion of women had doubled to over 12 females to every 10 males. By comparison, the Hokkien, the largest dialect group, had a female/male ratio of around 9 : 10.

There was a variety of jobs available on arrival. Prostitution, previously the most 'popular' occupation for single women, especially in Singapore, became less viable an option once the bans on prostitution and brothels took effect. By 1931, domestic service had become the most popular female occupation among the Chinese in Singapore. The 1931 Census lists just under 7,000 females being employed as domestic servants (including work in hotels), far outstripping every other occupation—agriculture was next with around 1,200. Admittedly, prostitution was not one of the listed occupations. Perhaps it was included under the heading of 'No Gainful Employment' which recorded over 110,000 females in that category. The new immigrants in the 1930s greatly swelled the number of women in domestic service in Singapore. By the next census in 1947, just under 15,500 women were working in private domestic service, easily the most popular female occupation. The next two were hawking, with around 4,000, and agriculture with just under 3,000.

Malaya, on the other hand, offered a greater variety of employment, predominantly in agriculture, mining, and rubber estates, where the majority of the Cantonese were to be found, especially in the states of Perak and Selangor. With the world's richest tin deposits, the Kinta Valley in Perak had, from the very beginning, attracted the Cantonese. When economic conditions began to improve in the mid-1930s, mine and estate owners faced a shortage of labour due to the earlier repatriation of the men, and with restrictions on male immigration still in effect, they had to import women to do the work. In Perak and Selangor in 1947, around 17,000 women worked in agriculture, another 17,000 as rubber tappers, and just over 6,000 women in mining. Although not

23 Women hawkers.
Another popular Chinese female occupation.
(Courtesy National Museum, Singapore)

numerically as popular as in Singapore, domestic service was still an attractive proposition in affluent urban areas with large Chinese populations—like Penang, Ipoh, and Kuala Lumpur. A total of just under 13,000 women were recorded as being employed as domestic servants in Penang, Perak, and Selangor.

It was during this period in the 1930s that the majority of women who became amahs arrived in Singapore and Malaya. Although no figures were kept, it was estimated that the same was true of Hong Kong. There had, of course, been amahs in all these countries since the mid-nineteenth century. It would, however, probably be true to say that many of the early amahs in Singapore and Malaya were not Cantonese. Thus, the 1930s could be considered as the start of the era of the Cantonese amah in the Far East.

Although the vast majority of Cantonese women left as a consequence of hardship, this was not always the case. Some left, according to Ow Ah Tim, because they 'no longer wanted to work in the fields and left for easier work abroad' and not apparently due to the shortage of work in China. A few, like her, had previously worked as domestic servants before they left; she had been one for sixteen years in Shanghai but left with the onset of the Sino-Japanese War in 1937. Most of the women, however, came directly from a rural life.

Once the women had decided to leave, the main difficulties facing them were the travel arrangements. To many who had been no further than Canton, this would have been a major problem. Fortunately, most were able to avail themselves of the expert services of a man known as a *sui haak* (literally, 'water guest'). He was usually a sailor, ex-sailor or trader familiar with travel arrangements and immigration regulations and had knowledge of the country the emigrants were travelling to. He advised them on all relevant matters and even lent them money on occasions. It was usual for him to come from the same district, and even the same village as the emigrant amahs accompanying him. Tang Pui Yin describes him as a sort of 'tour leader'. He was also a great deal more—a trusted friend, an adviser and confidant in a strange country. To many new emigrants, he was an essential link. On return trips, he often acted as a courier, taking back goods or money to relatives as well as accompanying some of them back on visits to their families.

A woman intending to emigrate would usually seek out a *sui haak* or, should he need the business, he would go round offering

24 Early portrait of baby amah and child in Singapore.
This photograph, taken in the early 1900s,
shows a Chinese amah in typical dress of the period.
(Courtesy National Museum, Singapore)

his services. Once a price was agreed on, he made all the necessary arrangements. If several women from the same village wanted to emigrate, as was common, they received a 'group discount'.

I got in touch with a *sui haak* from my village and came over with him and *chi mui* [sisters] from my village. I paid him $10. We went from Canton to Hong Kong first and from there to Singapore. The fare was about $30. This included food and the journey took four to five days. (Lau Siew Yong.)

Those who did not go with a *sui haak* usually accompanied relatives or friends back.

My family were silk weavers but as business was bad I decided to leave. A friend of mine in the next village was returning to Singapore and told me all about it. She offered to take me back with her, if I was interested. I was glad to go.

We went from our village to Canton and then to Hong Kong and from there to Singapore. We bought our tickets from an agency. From what I remember, no documents were necessary except for a piece of paper which allowed you to go. (Leong Siew Kee.)

Travelling as deck passengers, which they all did, was invariably uncomfortable, the degree of discomfort being dependent on the ship itself and on the prevailing climatic conditions.

On arrival at the ports, they were interviewed by immigration officials and officers from the Chinese Protectorate. The first group were interested only in entry formalities while the latter were specifically concerned that the girls and women had not been duped into coming. Should they be single, young, and without a local sponsor, they would automatically be put in the Po Leung Kuk until one was found and a job provided. If this was not possible, they remained there until they were of age and could be married off.

I arrived at the docks in 1936 and was interviewed by an officer from the Chinese Protectorate. He had a Chinese interpreter to translate for him. I was asked if there was anyone to meet me. My *Ah Koo* (aunt) was supposed to meet me but she was not there. I showed them a photo of her but as she was not there to vouch for me, I was taken to the Po Leung Kuk, where I had to wear a uniform and do housework like the other girls.

Luckily for me, the *sui haak* who brought me over had my aunt's address and went to tell her what had happened. She got a shopkeeper to sponsor me. I spent a week there and was only allowed to leave after the guarantee was received and my aunt had found me a job as a *yat keok tek* [all-purpose maid]. A man from the Po Leung Kuk came to check on me at my place of work and I had to report back there once a month for a year. (Lui Wai Foon.)

Arrival in the new country was not always a happy occasion. Ho Ah Yuet remembers that she did not want to emigrate: 'I was depressed and scared when I arrived. I knew no one here and my mother had just died. I had only a few belongings and very little money. Although I had a relative here who was sponsoring me, I had never met her.'

Most, however, were met by someone they already knew—a relative, friend, or 'sister'. With the trauma of departure and the discomfort of travel over, they were pleased to come, excited at the prospect of a new life for themselves and hopeful of a better one for their families in China.

CANTONESE AMAHS

The archetypal Cantonese amah, instantly recognizable in her distinctive black and white dress.

(Courtesy Hong Kong Government)

25 The baby amah, Singapore, 1941.
Most famous of the amahs.
(Courtesy Joanna Wormald)

7

FROM UNSOILED HANDS TO 'ONE-LEG-KICK'

CHINESE female domestic servants are universally known as 'amahs', yet the origin of the term is by no means clear. According to the *Oxford English Dictionary*, the word 'amah' is an Anglo-Indian term coined in 1839 meaning 'wet nurse' and derived from the Portuguese word for nurse, *ama*. *Chamber*'s extends it to mean 'native maidservant or child's nurse, especially wet-nurse', again giving the Portuguese *ama* as the source. *Webster*'s is more expansive and precise. It not only gives the Portuguese source of *ama*—wet-nurse—but also states that that term itself comes from the Medieval Latin *amma*. Furthermore, it defines 'amah' as meaning 'a female servant typically Chinese, especially a nurse'. *An English-Chinese Standard Dictionary* published in 1908 in Shanghai by the Commercial Press Ltd., however, gives the term as being Chinese in origin and derived from *nai ma*—literally meaning 'milk-mother', i.e. wet-nurse. Local sources attribute 'amah' as being derived from '*ma ma*', the term used by Chinese children in addressing their mother. Thus, a servant who took the place of their mother in looking after them was addressed as '*ah ma*'. And as women who looked after babies or children were the most common type of female servant, this was later adopted by the British as the term for all Chinese female servants and re-spelt as 'amah'.

A more contemporary explanation of the term comes from *Things Chinese*, edited by T. C. Lai, and published in 1979 in Hong Kong by the Swindon Book Company. It offers an interesting insight into the social origins of the word and links the movement against discrimination of women started in the middle of the nineteenth century with the existence of the amahs. It states that a number of women grouped themselves into coteries by swearing themselves to a life of chastity as well as organizing themselves to be household servants, later called amahs. A later

26 Early baby amahs in Hong Kong.

Wood-engraving titled 'Chinese Nursemaids on the Parade-ground, Hong Kong'
taken from the *Illustrated London News*, 17 October 1857.
(Courtesy Wellcome Institute Library, London)

account reveals that this practice originated in South Kwangtung and, perhaps, due to this link, the word became synonymous with Cantonese domestic servants. As used in Singapore, Malaya, and Hong Kong, the word 'amah' largely followed this definition with the difference that amahs did not have to be single or celibate, although often the case.

'Amah' here, therefore, simply means Cantonese female domestic servant. It should not be confused with another Anglo-Indian term, 'ayah', which means 'A native Indian nurse or lady's maid' (*Oxford English Dictionary*). The term 'amah', however, was not used by everyone. It was employed predominantly by the English-speaking part of the population, whether expatriate or local, as well as by the Baba Chinese and local non-Chinese races. In Hong Kong, where the population is almost entirely Cantonese, the terms used were *kung yan*, literally 'worker' but meaning 'servant' here, and *ma cheh*. These were also used by the Cantonese in Singapore and Malaya. Other Chinese groups have their own terms for 'servant'. Cantonese servants invariably referred to themselves as *kung yan* and the work they did as *chi ka kung* or 'family work', i.e. domestic service.

While 'amah' and *kung yan* are terms generally describing Cantonese servants, *ma cheh* applied only to a particular group of amahs. As far as the general public and most employers were concerned, all Cantonese servants who were dressed in the distinctive 'uniform' of black trousers and white *samfoo* top were known as *ma cheh*. The servants themselves, and knowledgeable employers, however, only used the term to describe a particular group of 'black and white' Cantonese servants. These were single women from Shun Tak who had taken vows never to marry. They were called *ma cheh* as it is a Shun Tak term and originally used to refer to single women who had taken such vows. When applied to amahs, it had a more specific meaning. The first word, *ma* or 'mother', comes from '*ah ma*', the term used by Chinese children in addressing the servant who looked after them, while the second word, *cheh* or 'older sister', used in reference to amahs denotes spinsterhood. Thus *ma cheh* simply means 'spinster servant'. The women were proud to be called *cheh* as they viewed spinsterhood as being synonymous with purity.

Many of these women were previously silk workers in Shun Tak and as such, they would have led a more independent life-style than most of their contemporaries from the Pearl River Delta. It was hardly surprising, therefore, that they were

27 *Ma cheh* in a goldsmith's shop.
The *ma cheh*: distinguished by their refined mannerisms, dress,
and hair-style—a loosely tied plait.
(Courtesy Hong Kong Government)

different from the other amahs—distinguished as much by their appearance and behaviour as by the domestic jobs they did.

Sarah Chin recalls that 'they always seemed to be young and pretty'. Adds Lim Bee Lum, 'The material for their clothes was more expensive, such as lawn and voile for the tops and satin for the trousers.' Mary Ong continues: 'It's hard to explain, but they were simply more stylish, more "classy". Instead of clogs or slippers, they would wear shoes, the slip-on Chinese type, and their hair was always beautifully oiled.' Their hair-style also distinguished them from other amahs. While others wore their hair either plaited tightly or coiled into a bun at the back of the head, the *ma cheh* would normally wear theirs in a single loose plait or occasionally unplaited.

The general consensus of opinion was that they were more relaxed, less severe, and more 'stylish'. According to Tang Pui Yin, 'their mannerisms were more uninhibited'. Mary Ong adds, 'They were usually for show as they had elegant manners and were often used by their mistresses to collect friends for a game of mahjong. Their status was such that they would frequently sit with the guests and would object to being told off for doing so.' Lui Wai Foon, from Tung Koon, offers an amah's view with a certain wry admiration: '*Ma cheh* are Shun Tak women. They work for hostesses, "service" flats, and prostitutes. They also worked as baby amahs for rich Chinese as well as for Europeans. They wear their hair in a plait and are better-dressed.' She adds that the *ma cheh* considered themselves superior as they only did jobs which 'did not soil their hands'. Consequently, other amahs often disapproved of them, due as much to their choice of work as to their snobbishness. In Singapore and Malaya, they were also known as *amah cheh*.

The Cantonese amahs were involved in three main areas of domestic activity: minding the children, cooking, and household work. The one looking after the children was the *chow tsai* or baby amah. The cook was known as the *chi fun* and usually did the marketing as well. The household amah or the *ta chup* would be responsible for the cleaning, tidying, washing, and ironing. If she only did the laundry, she was known as a *sai tong*. However, if only a single amah was employed, as was usual in less well-to-do homes, she would have to do all the work in the household, i.e. cooking, marketing, and all the household tasks (including minding the children at times). She was known as a *yat keok tek*, the literal translation of which is 'one-leg-kick'.

28 Hong Kong baby amah in the 1930s.
The terrain of Hong Kong made 'piggy-back' carrying of infants more practical
than prams or push-chairs. Only local children were usually carried this way.
(Courtesy Hong Kong Government)

The word 'amah' is a noun and not a form of address, thus it was both incorrect and impolite to address a servant as such. In Kwangtung, a mother was called '*lo ma*' (old mother) by people who did not know her. Those who knew her would address her as the mother of so-and-so, for example, if her son was Mr Leong, she would be known as 'Leong *ma*'—mother of Mr Leong. As servants in China were usually married, these were the forms of address used.

Most of the Cantonese amahs abroad, however, were unmarried; thus, these forms fell out of use and a variety of terms took their place. Ho It Chong, in his academic exercise, 'The Cantonese Domestic Amahs', stated that in order to give the younger servants a place in the social group, it was 'considered polite to address them as so-and-so *cheh*, i.e. older sister'. *Cheh* was also the honorific term used by Chinese employers as it accorded them a certain position and respect in the family. Thus, for example, if an amah's name was Lui Wai Foon ('Lui' being the surname), she would be addressed as 'Foon *cheh*' with the surname omitted and end name used (or sometimes the middle name) by 'sisters' or friends about her own age or younger. The older women would call her 'Ah Foon' or even 'Foon *cheh*' if she was liked and respected.

As far as the employers were concerned, the more traditional Chinese families would call her 'Foon *cheh*', while others would address her as 'Ah Foon'. Non-Chinese local families together with the expatriates would usually call her 'Ah Foon'. Occasionally, she would simply be called by name, i.e. 'Wai Foon'. In general, the forms of address most widely used were 'Foon *cheh*' and 'Ah Foon'.

29 Typical Chinatown buildings.

The amahs' *coolie fong*, until fairly recently,
were commonly located in buildings such as these.
(Courtesy National Museum, Singapore)

8

LIVING WITH SISTERS;
WORKING FOR STRANGERS

THE first priority on arrival was accommodation. Fortunately for most, it was not a problem as their relatives, friends or *chi mui* would find them accommodation in the building in which they themselves were staying. *Chi mui* were unmarried women who were friends and had pledged to treat each other like real sisters.

The young newcomers from China, dressed in black, would undoubtedly have been pleased to be with their own kind again. If they arrived in Singapore but their destination was in Malaya, they would be taken there by train. They could, of course, have gone directly to Malayan ports such as Penang. The amahs' accommodation was known as a *kongsi uk* (shared house) or *kongsi fong* (shared room). It was also called a *fong tsai* (small room) in Malaya or *coolie fong* (worker's room) in Singapore. This was a room or a set of rooms in predominantly Chinese districts.

Arriving in Hong Kong was far less of a shock as many had relatives here. Those without relatives would also be taken by their 'sisters' to their accommodation, known locally as a *chi mui fong* (sisters' room) and located in the cheaper districts of Hong Kong.

At the *coolie fong* (for simplicity, this term, the most widely used in Singapore, will also generally be used to describe the amahs' accommodation, whether in Malaya or Hong Kong), she would be shown her bunk and the place to store her few belongings.

The *coolie fong* was the focal point of these women—a home, a gathering place, a social club—a unique place and greatly valued by them, despite the grime and dirt and impossibly crowded conditions. There was surprisingly little disagreement among its inhabitants; a sense of order usually prevailed. Amahs who disliked their *coolie fong* for any reason would simply leave for another. Amahs belonging to the same 'sister' group would leave together.

Reasons for leaving were usually either personal difficulties with other tenants or because they had found something better.

In Singapore and Malaya, these rooms were generally located in two- or three-storey terraced colonial-style dwellings of plastered brick and timber. In popular commercial districts, there would usually be shops on the ground floor with the accommodation above. In less busy areas, the entire building would be used as accommodation with the ground floor serving as the communal area for eating and cooking and the floor(s) above as the sleeping quarters. These houses had narrow frontages about 4 m wide and stretching back 15–25 m. As can be imagined, the interiors were dark and dingy with the dirt and grime becoming ingrained into the fabric of the building over the years, the walls looking as if they had not been repainted since the houses were first built. Access to the upper floors was via unlit, steep wooden stairs with narrow treads. It is not difficult to imagine the hundreds of amahs who would have stayed in these shabby surroundings over the years, their experiences etched into the woodwork and walls.

Each floor was subdivided into several cubicles and there could be as many as six cubicles per floor with up to six occupants in each. The cubicles furthest away from the windows were depressingly dark and the usual single bare bulb did little to lighten the gloom. Occasionally, there would be an internal light well which helped to illuminate the dismal interiors. Each floor, therefore, could have up to thirty-six tenants, making a total of between seventy and eighty tenants in the larger houses. Not all the inhabitants were amahs. Sometimes they shared the house with others, including factory workers, hawkers, and even families.

Pre-war, the rent was between 70 cts. and $1 per month, and more recently about $20 per month, and paid either directly to the owner or, more commonly, to the chief tenant of the house or to the principal tenant of each floor, as in Hong Kong. In return, they were provided with a wooden bunk and a space to store their belongings, either under the bunk or on shelves alongside. Ablutive and cooking facilities were usually found at the rear of the building.

No *coolie fong* was without its altar, usually dedicated to one of the traditional Chinese gods; Kwan Yin was a particular favourite. Furniture was sparse. Other than the bunks and shelves, there would only be an occasional wooden table, a few stools or chairs, and perhaps a small cupboard or two. Food was often kept suspended from the ceiling in bamboo or wicker baskets. The

30 The interior of a _coolie fong_.
Cluttered, crowded, and dingy—but it was _home_.
(Photograph the author)

only decoration on the walls were usually framed black and white photographs of themselves, relatives, or 'sisters'. The portraits were always stylized with simple props and a painted backdrop, usually depicting a tranquil scene. In common with emigrants the world over, photographs of themselves were often taken to send home to families. To create a good impression, jewellery would be painted on the photographs if they themselves had none.

The chief tenant, usually an older woman who could no longer work, was provided with free accommodation in return for collecting the rent and keeping the place clean. After every tenant's share was collected, there would normally be a surplus which she could keep. It was, however, not a popular job as rent-collecting, particularly in a house with many tenants, was not easy.

In the larger *coolie fong*, it was rare for the women to know each other as they were seldom all there at the same time. It was only on occasions like the Chinese New Year when most would turn up. Generally, they visited it on their off-days, to check for mail and to have a welcome chat with whichever of their 'sisters' were present. Popular games played were mahjong or *tin kau*, a variation of dominoes.

In Hong Kong, the *chi mui fong* were located in anonymous three- to four-storey tenement buildings. Each floor was similarly divided into cubicles. Unlike the situation in Malaya and Singapore, where the entire floor would usually be occupied by amahs, the cubicles on each floor were frequently shared by an assortment of people, including families. With the premium on space in the colony, conditions were invariably more crowded.

Despite the communal sharing of the premises, the amahs always remained individuals, as demonstrated by their habit of cooking and eating their food separately. This practice continued even after they had retired to a Vegetarian House.

Despite the extremely crowded and primitive conditions, the *coolie fong* had several advantages. It was a place to stay when they were not working, whether unemployed or between jobs, to visit on days off, and where they could rest during periods of minor illness. They could also live there before going to and after returning from China. Being able to store their belongings there enabled them to take only the barest of necessities with them when they lived-in. Having a permanent address for contact and correspondence made it easier to find employment. There was the added security of being with their own kind and in the event of death,

31 Portrait of two *chi mui*.
Taken to send home, it occupies pride of place in their *coolie fong*.
Notice the painted-on jewellery.
(Courtesy Tong Mern Sern Antiques, Singapore)

there was the knowledge that their 'sisters' would make the necessary arrangements—an important consideration. Above all, it was their *home*.

Outside of China, this was the only home they ever had. Although shared with many others, they only paid a comparatively small sum for all the advantages it offered. It was a genuine community and provided a definite sense of belonging. Leong Ah Hoe remembers her early days in her *coolie fong* with much affection: 'There were several tens of us staying together. When we came back after work, we would talk and tell stories. How happy we were!' In the less affluent times of the 1930s and 1940s, many did not live-in at their employers' homes but returned each evening to their *coolie fong*.

Some have had the same *coolie fong* since their arrival. Lee Ah Yew has 'lived' in the same one since she first came sixty years ago. Others moved from time to time. Lok Ah Kew explains the reasons for these moves: 'I left when my *chi mui* left. We went when we found a more comfortable place, for example, when the room was more spacious and the kitchen and bathroom better, etc.'

In more recent years, many had to move because the houses were pulled down for redevelopment. Thus, many historically interesting houses in Chinatown and elsewhere have disappeared. In Singapore, the ones who can afford to do so, either because they have sufficient savings or through the generosity of their ex-employers, club together to rent or sometimes even to buy a small government flat—the modern equivalent of a *coolie fong* and usually shared between two to four women. Most are retired. Although physical conditions are better—improved sanitation, better cooking facilities as well as lighting—the flat lacks a sense of community and security, being located in multi-tenanted anonymous blocks. The front door, with its several locks, is symptomatic of the times, quite unlike the open doorways of their Chinatown *coolie fong*. But, perhaps as a result of habit, sentiment, lack of space, or a combination of all, their belongings are stacked in exactly the same way as in their old *coolie fong*—under the bed and along the wall.

Once accommodation had been settled, the critical task of obtaining employment had to be attended to. Over the years, most jobs were obtained as a result of personal recommendation. An amah in work would recommend her 'sister' or relative for a job. This method worked very well, for the simple reason that no

32 Houses due for demolition.

A typical row of neglected Chinatown houses
soon to be demolished for urban re-development.
(Photograph the author)

amah would ever recommend a 'dud' as her own reputation would suffer; and in turn, any amah recommended by a 'sister' or relative would feel obligated not to let her down.

In later years, when amahs were in short supply, this process of recommendation took an interesting turn. Employers, instead of amahs, had to be recommended. Joan Oliphant, whose husband was Deputy Chief Manager of the Hongkong and Shanghai Bank in Hong Kong, remembers:

We got Ah Siew through a friend's amah. We all got them through other amahs. It was not easy to get a really good amah. One had to be recommended. When we went to Hong Kong (from Singapore), Ah Siew accompanied us there but she did not want to stay, and through a relative of hers, found us Ah Choi. It wasn't a question of Ah Choi being recommended to me; rather, the other way around. Apparently Ah Siew had told her that I was a good mistress as I helped to look after the children. Six years later, Ah Choi said to me, "Peak side [a prestigious residential area in Hong Kong] only got three good missies, Mrs Richardson, Mrs Bennett and you." I was greatly honoured! Most expatriate wives would play bridge all day, come home and go to bed in the afternoon and then go out all night leaving everything to the amah.

In Singapore, a less widespread method of obtaining servants was via employment agencies, resorted to mainly by expatriates, particularly those new to the country. These agencies were found in areas familiar and accessible to Europeans and close to popular *coolie fong* locations. The amahs would come in the morning and sit in the waiting room, where prospective employers would look them over before making their selection. In Malaya, the employment agency sometimes shared the same building as the *coolie fong*. The amahs who used these agencies usually did so because they had no friends, relatives, or 'sisters' to recommend them. These agencies generally vanished with the British withdrawal from the area.

Other methods were used to obtain employment. Advertising was a popular method in the early days, not in newspapers but at the *coolie fong* itself. A board would be placed outside the house and on it would be written a list of the jobs being sought. Prospective employers needing a servant would go to the areas where the *coolie fong* were located. If a cook, for example, was needed and there were several women wanting such a job, the accepted practice was that the one who had been longest unemployed would be interviewed first and so on. It was a civilized and orderly system. Employers requiring a specific type of servant would make their own enquiries. Leong Ah Hoe explains, 'Some employers would want to hire a newly arrived immigrant from China as they would be cheaper.' These methods were used mainly by less well-to-do Chinese.

Employment agencies were more popular in Hong Kong than in Singapore or Malaya and, again, used predominantly by middle- and low-income families. 'Employment agency' is perhaps too grand a term used with regard to the Hong Kong situation. It implies a formal set-up—an office dealing only in matters of employment. In reality, these employment agencies were informal affairs—'usually street stalls (not shops) near food markets', according to Eva Lo. An amah seeking employment would go to the stall and inform the stall-holder of the kind of job she wanted. This would then be written in Chinese on a board and displayed. The stall-holder would arrange for her to be interviewed by interested employer(s). She would then go to the address of her prospective employer(s) to discuss pay, duties, and conditions. If she was satisfied, she would accept the job and a date for starting work arranged.

According to Ho It Chong, pay was initially set by the women themselves, the 'sister' group agreeing on an average wage. Two other factors affected pay: (1) her employer—whether expatriate or local, and (2) the type of job she held. Expatriates or Europeans usually paid higher salaries than local employers. Generally, there was a difference in salary of about 50 per cent:

	1930s	*1950s*
European	$8-15	$130-170
Local	$5-10	$ 90-120

It should be pointed out that although expatriate employers paid more, they rarely supplied food. Many servants maintained that having to purchase food out of their own pockets greatly reduced the apparent disparity between the two groups and made the net sum earned roughly similar. The type of job also determined the wages received. Average pay in the mid-1950s were:

	European Employer	*Local Employer*
Cook (*Chi Fun*)	$150	$110
Baby Amah (*Chow Tsai*)	$130	$ 90
Household Amah (*Ta Chup*)	$110	$ 80

There was, of course, considerable variation between individual employers. Also, an amah who did a combination of jobs would be paid more than one who only did a single job.

In the early years, the important considerations when seeking employment were wages, nature of work, size of family, size of dwelling, and their accommodation. Hours of work, time off, or holidays were seldom discussed and increments were mentioned only after they were employed, never at the time of the interview. Tang Ah Thye elaborates:

The important things in any new job were, well, the basic things: How many in the family and what I had to do. Did I shop as well as cook? Did I do all the washing? How much could I spend on food each day? Where do I sleep and so on. I liked to make that all clear. Most important—salary. Working hours were never discussed as that depended on how fast you worked.

Although wages were considered most important at the time of the interview, the type of employer/family was usually regarded as being more significant once they were employed. This attitude is confirmed by Phyllis Tan, a lawyer in Singapore: 'Ah Peng, our cook, was much sought after and could easily have got another job with higher pay. In fact, some so-called friends tried unsuccessfully to entice her away.' For many, this sense of loyalty was their most memorable quality.

On the whole, they were not unduly concerned about conditions of work, as jobs were much the same whoever they worked for. Comments Kwan Ah Sap, 'Conditions of work? What conditions of work? Work is work.' Chinese employers always provided full board and lodging while other local and European employers normally provided only lodgings. Hours of work were seldom fixed in Chinese and local households. Work would start at daybreak, around 6 a.m., and considered completed only after the last meal had been eaten and dishes cleaned, unless they had a specific job with specific hours. This happened only in very wealthy households employing several amahs. It was also the norm in most expatriate homes and accounts for the reason why many amahs preferred working for European families. In the words of Leong Ah Pat: 'I preferred to work for Europeans—they had specific working hours and specific jobs. Chinese employers would ask you to do all sorts of things at all times.' Leong Siew Kee also preferred working for expatriate families:

European employers are much better. They don't order you about and you have more freedom with them. Missy Oliphant was one employer who was very considerate. She provided me with everything I needed—scissors, clothes, etc. I always offered to pay but she wouldn't accept it. She understood my Chinese customs well.

Together with the higher salaries generally paid by expatriate employers, better living quarters, specific conditions and hours of work were the characteristic features of what the amahs called *hong mo kung* (European work). The disadvantages, in the eyes of those who did not like working for them, were that they had to provide their own food as well as cope with an entirely different life-style. 'I didn't like the idea of working for Europeans. You'd have to bring your pots and pans along to do your own cooking. Also rice, oil, etc. It's like a major move. Also, I didn't understand their language. I just didn't like working for them in spite of higher salaries,' reveals Tang Ah Thye.

Another aspect of 'European work' was the wearing of the black and white 'uniform'. All expatriate employers expected their amahs to wear black trousers and a white *samfoo* (Chinese-style) top, especially the baby amahs. Those in Hong Kong usually required their amahs to wear black slip-on Chinese shoes as well. This was also true of most well-to-do local employers. It was slightly less formal in Singapore and Malaya: black and white was the expected style of dress but slippers rather than shoes could be worn. In fact, the familiar black and white dress of the amahs has been attributed to the British. They liked their servants to look neat and to have a recognizable uniform—to be identifiably 'servants'. This style of dress started some time between the two World Wars and soon became the characteristic dress of most Cantonese amahs. They were then known simply as the 'black and white', particularly in Singapore and Malaya.

Many Chinese-speaking employers, particularly the less wealthy, did not insist on this style of dress. Black trousers would still be worn but the tops would usually be a pale colour (light blue was popular); sometimes they were patterned. Wan Yong Gui recollects:

My employer wanted me to wear black and white dress, so I wore black and white. Servants who worked for non-Baba Chinese families, wore either white tops or blue tops with dots like white pepper. If you worked for foreigners, you had to wear white top and black trousers. Cantonese employers were not concerned about dress, so we wore what we liked.

Many families who did not mind what the servants wore when they were cooking or doing the household chores would insist that black and white be worn on formal or special occasions, or when guests were present. The amahs themselves rarely wore white from choice. On days off and for festive occasions, the tops would be in pale pastel shades, often with a faint flowery pattern.

Most local employers gave their servants little time off. The usual pattern was to allow them time off on the first and fifteenth days of the lunar month (i.e. the new and full moon). They would none the less normally have to complete their work before leaving. A cook, for example, could leave only after the mid-day meal had been prepared and had to return in time to prepare the evening meal. They also had major festival days, like the Chinese New Year, off; but if they worked for Chinese families, they were usually not allowed to leave until the third day of the New Year as they were required to help with family festivities. At other times, they would ask for time off when needed. As these requests were few and far between, they were normally granted. Holidays as such were a foreign concept to them and considered unimportant. The only extended period off they would want would be for visits to China. In such circumstances, they would always find a 'sister' as a temporary replacement before they left. This had a two-fold purpose—it demonstrated loyalty to their employer and ensured that their job would be there when they returned. No 'sister' would ever consider supplanting her, even if requested to do so by the employer.

Changing conditions in later years, together with the shortage of amahs, meant that an amah could make greater demands, such as more time off, clothing to be supplied, and radio or television to be provided. In return, however, employers usually received excellent service and total commitment.

Thus, although their employers were strangers at first, many became so attached to the families they served, that they would work for them as long as they were required—often till the day they retired. This was due both to a sense of loyalty to the families and to their own need for security. Often, an amah became so completely involved with the family that children would say with a mixture of exasperation and affection, 'She's worse than our mother!'

The most common reason given for leaving an employer was his unreasonableness or bad temper. 'I would change jobs only because I could not get on with them—never about salary,' said

Tang Ah Thye. This was a common response. Other reasons included ill-health or their services no longer being required. Pay or conditions of work were not often given as reasons for leaving.

For many amahs, their first job was as an all-purpose amah or *yat keok tek*. For doing all the household jobs in the 1930s, they would have been paid between $5 and $10 a month, with meals provided. Some early experiences of work recalled:

I was paid $5 a month in my first job. I worked as a *yat keok tek* for two ladies who were running a school. I had to do everything. I stayed there for about a year. My next job was working for a family of nine persons, again as a *yat keok tek*, for which I was paid $8 a month. I worked from five in the morning till nine at night. (Leong Ah Pat.)

My first job was working for a Cantonese family as a *yat keok tek*. My aunt found me the job. I worked for them for two years and my pay was $10 a month. (Lui Wai Foon.)

It took me a long time before I got my first job—as a *yat keok tek*. It was with a taxi-driver who had six children. I slept with the children and sometimes the children wet themselves at night and I would be soaked! I received $6 a month. I stayed there for two years. I left as pay was not enough to repay my debts—money I borrowed when I was not working. I then went to work for a Cantonese as a *chow tsai* (baby amah) and was paid $12 a month. (Ho Ah Yuet.)

It took me 1-2 months before I got my first job. My *chi mui* found me the job. I cannot remember exactly how much I was paid, but it was less than $10 a month. My employer was Cantonese and I worked as a *sai tong* (washerwoman). (Leong Hock Kam.)

After I came, it took 10-20 days before I was employed. Someone staying at the same *coolie fong* as myself got it for me. All the women staying there worked as domestic servants. I worked as a *yat keok tek* and was paid $5 a month. I stayed for two to three months. (Tang Ah Thye.)

I got my first job after two weeks. I swept the floor, cleaned the spittoons and helped the cook. The family were Baba Chinese and they only spoke Malay. As I didn't understand Malay, the washerwoman had to interpret for me. The pay was $8 a month. (Wan Yong Gui.)

In the early years, there was a great deal of movement between jobs, due primarily to the amahs adjusting to a new environment and getting accustomed to domestic work itself. Few had previously worked as servants and the only domestic experience they had was helping their mothers at home. It should not be forgotten that almost all of them came from a rural environment, with no

33 Raffles Place, Singapore, 1920s.
Sophisticated Singapore, a far cry from the simple peasant environment
of the amahs' home in the Pearl River Delta.
(Courtesy National Museum, Singapore)

electricity, tap water, or cars, and few large buildings. They were all undoubtedly pleased to be in employment but once they became accustomed to the work and the life-style, they became more selective.

The Second World War was a difficult time for everyone, not least for the amahs themselves. Servants, in general, had to be dispensed with. The ones who were no longer employed either returned to their *coolie fong* or moved to areas considered safer. Some stayed loyally with their employers throughout the war, even though they were not paid. This was partly due to the fact that they themselves had nowhere to go. The main reason, however, appeared to be their strong sense of devotion to their employers.

Some amahs who were no longer employed simply adapted to the different circumstances. Some turned to selling vegetables or small-goods, while others became hawkers. Leong Siew Kee remembers, 'I had no job during the war, so I sold bread and cigarettes. I did this until the liberation. On the whole, the Japanese left us alone. I had a little stall next to the Chinese Hospital and made quite good money—Japanese notes, of course, but enough to live on.' Many others, much better-off than themselves, were crushed by the hardships of war. The amahs' stoicism, enterprise, and resilience—the very qualities which made them ideal emigrants—also helped them to survive.

After the war, conditions gradually improved and many were reunited with their former employers. By the start of the 1950s, they were fully established and for the next three decades, Cantonese amahs completely dominated the domestic service field and confirmed their reputation as being the very finest servants.

34 The ubiquitous baby amah.
Helping out at a birthday party.
(Courtesy Felice Coombs)

9

A DAY IN THE LIFE

AMAHS were employed only in 'indoor' domestic work. Outdoor jobs such as gardening and chauffeuring were male occupations, though there were some amahs who voluntarily helped in the garden and looked after family pets and even farmyard animals. Dorothy Chang recollects,

Ah Fong loved gardening and had very green fingers, so she grew everything, including fruit and vegetables. As she became very fond of animals, she looked after all the menagerie including doctoring the poultry when they got ill. I remember her pulling maggots out of the goose's wing when that got infected.

As domestic labour was cheap and households large, many families, particularly in Singapore and Malaya, were able to employ a servant for each of the main household activities—cooking, looking after children, and household work. In wealthy households, there were even servants to attend to the needs of individual family members, the baby amah being the most common. Each child would have his or her own amah. In Hong Kong, a familiar figure in such households was the personal maid to the mistress. Kwan Ah Sap recalls her early years:

I started as a general maid, picking up and tidying up. Then I progressed to being a personal maid. Well, you served one person and followed that person everywhere. Sometimes, I was personal maid to a newly married girl—like a bridal maid. I washed and ironed her clothes, cleaned her room, helped her dress and so on. I didn't have to cook or do anything else—just do the lady's work and take care of her. It wasn't very difficult or strenuous.

The cook would sometimes have someone helping with the preparation and the washing-up. Household work was divided between cleaning, sweeping, and tidying on one hand, and the laundry, i.e. washing and ironing, on the other. Furthermore, if it was a large house, there would probably be a separate maid responsible for each floor.

A servant solely to attend to the needs of visitors and to serve food existed only in homes of the very rich or influential. This position, which was always filled by men, gradually vanished after the war. Such a servant was known as a 'houseboy'. He was, however, rarely a boy and frequently had a family. If he had children, they sometimes helped, boys with the serving and girls with the housework. Houseboys were usually Hainanese. They also had the reputation of being the best cooks and many households, before the war, would usually employ a Hainanese cook.

The majority of households, however, had only one or two servants. The all-purpose servant or *yat keok tek* was more prevalent in Hong Kong than in either Singapore or Malaya, partly because households there were generally less affluent, and partly because there was usually only room for one servant in their flats. As can be imagined, the 'one-leg-kick', known in Victorian England by the more descriptive title of 'maid-of-all-work', performed an exceptionally strenuous and difficult job. Tang Ah Thye worked as one for most of her working life:

I have mostly worked for Chinese families as a *yat keok tek*, which included cleaning, washing, ironing, cooking; in fact, everything except minding the children. Most of the families had around six to seven members. I woke up early in the morning around 5 a.m. and after getting myself ready, I would start getting breakfast. The master left for work after breakfast. After doing the dishes, I swept and cleaned the house from top to bottom. When that was done, I washed the clothes and prepared lunch, which the master would come back for. After clearing up, I did the ironing. When that was done, I took a bath. It would then be time to cook again. By the time dinner was over and I had cleared up and finished the dishes, it would be about 9 p.m. I would be free then.

This somewhat bland account conceals the tedious and arduous daily routine she performed seven days a week with only the occasional half-day off and typified the work of a 'one-leg-kick'. Kwan Ah Sap provides a contrast with her account of work with an English family:

I worked as a *yat keok tek* for an English military family of five. I didn't cook, they did it themselves, but I did everything else—cleaned, washed dishes, looked after the children and so on. I'd wake about 5 a.m., then start cleaning. Everything needed to be scrubbed and polished. It was really hard work. At about eight, they'd have their breakfast. The husband would then go to work. The two older ones would be at school and I would play with and look after the little one till about lunch-time, around one when the older children came home. I would prepare and give them their lunch. After lunch, the three-year-old took a nap while the older ones played by themselves. I would only then have time to cook and eat my own food. When that was over and the dishes had been done, I did the washing and the ironing. When the youngest one woke, I took all three for a walk to the Gardens and then back for dinner. The parents went out every night till about 2 or 3 a.m. and I was left looking after the children.

Often servants who started work in one capacity took on other duties as a result of shrinking households or through attachment to the family. Dorothy Chang describes how Ah Fong, the cook, became increasingly involved in other domestic duties. Although originally employed as a cook, she took on other duties and eventually ended up as a 'one-leg-kick'.

As it became harder to find maids who (a) were prepared to live-in, (b) were prepared to stay any length of time as opposed to filling in between jobs in factories and (c) weren't frightened by our dogs, she took on more and more tasks. She had always insisted on sweeping and cleaning the bedrooms—she said that both my parents were careless about money and jewellery and therefore, it would be putting temptation in the path of the maid—and she usually did the ironing as well. For the last ten years, she had taken to accompanying my mother on expeditions to the markets, then took over the marketing herself. She enjoyed bargaining and my mother hated marketing, so between them they were happy.

Loyalty may help to explain why they voluntarily chose to take on more work, but why should anyone working as a 'one-leg-kick' continue to do so when the job was so difficult? Tang Ah Thye explains:

I [have] always thought it better to put up with what I know than to make changes. I hate changing jobs. You can never tell if your next job wouldn't be worse. I also thought that if you only did one job, you'd have to work with other servants and [that] might lead to quarrels and other difficulties—better to do it all by myself. I am independent that way. I'd rather do it all, despite the hardship.

The difficulties she speaks of were very real, for not only did they have to work together for seven days a week, they had to live together as well. These problems became particularly relevant when a new amah was employed and had to work with a well-established older servant. Should another servant be required, the amah already in residence would normally be asked by her employer to find one. Inevitably she would recruit a younger one, often a relative or a 'sister'. In this way, she could maintain her premier status with the former and cordial relations with the latter, thus minimizing potential difficulties. Toh Ah Peng was employed as a cook in Phyllis Tan's family and when a *ta chup* was required, she recruited Ah Yee, a 'sister' from her *coolie fong*. Even though their jobs were theoretically separate, being 'sisters', they always helped each other whenever necessary.

This process of personal recommendation, probably more than any other, accounted for the remarkable fact that despite the close and continual contact between amahs working in the same household, there was comparatively little disagreement between them. The three amahs of Sarah Chin's family were invariably cheerful: 'They never sulked.' Despite the obvious advantages, there was one snag when getting one servant to recommend another. If the servant who had recommended the other was to leave for any reason other than to retire, it was incumbent on the other to leave with her—an unwritten rule among 'sisters'. This was the reason why some employers, like the author's mother, always took pains to employ their servants separately. 'I got Ah Woon (the baby amah) through one friend and Ah Foon (the cook) through another as I did not want to lose both of them, should either of them want to leave. Fortunately it did not happen. Both were excellent and worked well together.'

After the 'one-leg-kick', the next most arduous job was that of the *ta chup*. She was responsible for all the household work except cooking and looking after the children. Leong Siew Kee gives a graphic description of her job as a *ta chup*:

I worked for a large family, over twenty people in all—eleven children, the parents and the grandchildren. My job was to wash and iron, tidy and sweep, but not the living room. It was a large house, three storeys high. I used to do all the washing—clothes, dishcloths, sheets, towels, everything. I'd spend the whole morning washing, every day. Once a week, I'd wipe the floors and the stairs. On the days that I had to clean the floors I would not be able to finish my day's ironing. Luckily, I had an electric iron, not like the charcoal iron in the old days. [The reference here is to a hollow iron that had red-hot charcoal embers placed in it to heat it up, widely used until the 1950s.]

Although she laboured as a household maid towards the end of her working life, much of her earlier life was spent as a baby amah with expatriate families. Of all the different jobs done by the Cantonese amahs, it was their role as the *chow tsai* or baby amah that they are most associated with. Besides the marketing, other amahs were usually housebound. The baby amah, however, was ubiquitous. She accompanied her mistress on shopping expeditions, visits to friends or relations, trips to the beach, and even on holiday. She was ever-present when there were visitors to the home or when she helped with birthday parties. She was always around.

Baby amahs and their charges congregated in parks in the more salubrious parts of Singapore, Kuala Lumpur, Penang, Ipoh, and Hong Kong. These daily gatherings were a familiar sight in popular middle-class areas and were cheerful sessions eagerly looked forward to—a welcome break from the monotony of having to spend all day (as well as night, sometimes) looking after the children. Joan Oliphant reminisces, 'After breakfast, Ah Siew would take the baby and join the other amahs in a nearby park and gossip about their mistresses, etc. Fortunately, I had a happy marriage! There were no secrets at all. How can there be when you all stay in the same house?' Amahs working for expatriates tended to gossip more than those employed by local Chinese families. Of course, the amahs who were better treated would not gossip as much as those less well treated. Many who worked for the Chinese saw themselves as part of the families they served and thus, out of loyalty, would not gossip about them. 'They considered it their duty to protect the family and never gossiped about its members to anyone—not even their friends,' explains Lim Kian Leng. This did not apply to the expatriates who were not considered as 'family', although some amahs working for expatriate employers were exceptionally loyal.

Although not as strenuous as that of the household maid or as skilful as that of the cook, being responsible for the child's well-being virtually twenty-four hours a day made it possibly the most stressful of all the jobs. Her duties, usually, were to take complete care of him from the time he awoke to the time he went to bed, and if she slept in the same room—a common practice—to keep an eye on him at night as well. Leong Siew Kee elaborates: 'Even when I needed to go to the toilet, I had to get someone else to keep an eye on him, just in case he fell. I was always scared he would fall and would sit closer and closer. A lot of time was spent just keeping an eye on them (the baby and two older children). Time moves very slowly.'

After getting the child up in the morning and dressing him, she would give him breakfast. Sometimes, she had to prepare his meals as well, although this was usually done by the cook. Other

35 At the Botanic Gardens, Singapore, 1940.
Two baby amahs with their charges in the
Botanic Gardens, Singapore, a popular meeting place.
(Courtesy Joanna Wormald)

daily activities included taking him for walks, playing with him, bathing him, getting him toilet-trained, and ensuring that he behaved properly and came to no harm—in fact, apart from the mother's involvement in matters of discipline, she was completely responsible for him and spent considerably more time with him than his own mother did. As can be imagined, a very close bond often developed between amah and child and children brought up by doting amahs still hold them in much affection, even when they have grown up. Many were more attached to their amahs than to their own mothers. Some employers, however, were not too happy with this closeness. Ralph Coombs, an English engineer, felt that their baby amah, although excellent in most respects, was too obsessed with his youngest daughter. He remembers an occasion when they returned after a trip: 'Ah Fong greeted Celia and ignored everybody else, taking her immediately to the kitchen and giving her something to eat from her own food.' While amahs working for expatriate employers never viewed them as 'family', baby amahs, regardless of who they were working for, often regarded the child in their care as their own. When they were with other amahs, it was usual to hear them refer to the child as 'my son' or 'my daughter'; thus, in this case, it was clearly the act of a mother greeting her child.

Baby amahs with expatriate families followed more precise routines than those working for local employers. Leong Siew Kee recalls a typical day:

I worked as a baby amah only for Europeans in Singapore as well as in Malaya. The job was much the same for all the families. I always slept with the child. I'd wake about six, washed and cleaned myself. Then I'd wake him and take him to the toilet. Breakfast was next, milk made from milk powder. When I'd finished giving him his breakfast, I'd take him for a walk, then home for a bath around nine. After the bath, he would play while I had tea. He would then be taken to the toilet. The timing was definite. He would then play again, followed by a short nap.

While he was sleeping, I prepared my own meals and did bits of tidying up. I ate my own food which I bought for myself. Sometimes the cook bought it for me. After I cooked my food, I had to eat it hurriedly so as to be on time to feed the child. I would wake him around twelve, sometimes one, to give him his lunch, then back to the potty to train him. After playing for a little while, he would have another short nap while I had my bath.

When he woke at around three, he had orange juice, yes, orange juice every day. It would then be time to take him for a long walk. Usually I'd take an umbrella and walk to the flower gardens. There would be lots of baby amahs there. We would chat and around four, I brought him back. Then another bath before dinner. Always one in the morning and one in the evening. Dinner at around six was canned food usually—steamed meat and vegetables, you know, European things. After dinner, potty again and then got him ready for bed, about seven. Sometimes if he was very lively, he took some time settling down and I would have to wait until he was asleep before I could have my dinner; sometimes not till eight. I could not eat while looking after him.

After I had cooked and eaten my dinner, I would have a wash, do some sewing and go to bed around nine.

Although individual experiences vary, this account was typical of the baby amah's day in an expatriate household.

Wan Yong Gui enjoyed being a baby amah. She was employed by the Ongs, a Straits Chinese family in Singapore, and originally engaged because 'they wanted someone young to play with their son. An older person would not know how to play. I played lots of different games with him—football, five-stones, flew kites and so on. Older servants did not know how to do this.' Malay was the main language of communication. Although initially unable to speak Malay, her natural intelligence quickly allowed her to pick up the language.

We spoke in Malay. I listened and paid attention and remembered what my mistress said. After a while, I knew what different things were called. I couldn't speak well but I understood. The son spoke English to me. Like his mother, he pointed to things and said what their names were. He taught me English and I taught him Cantonese.

This linguistic exchange between amah and child was the main reason most non-Cantonese Chinese children learnt to speak Cantonese. In Singapore and Kuala Lumpur, the main mediums of communication used by Chinese employers with their amahs were Cantonese and Malay while in Penang, they were Hokkien and Malay. In Hong Kong, Cantonese was used exclusively by local employers. Expatriates in Singapore and Malaya spoke to their amahs in either pidgin English or Malay and in Hong Kong, only pidgin English was used. Thus, in Malaya and Singapore, European children were spoken to in either Malay or pidgin English, while in Hong Kong it was usually in pidgin English. Occasionally, Cantonese was used and some European children gained complete fluency in Cantonese as a result of the considerable time they spent with their amahs. Some amahs, like Foong Ah Chat, felt that 'it was not right to speak to them [the children] in Cantonese'. She herself became quite proficient in English after a lifetime's service with expatriate, mainly British, families.

Wan Yong Gui recalls some of her other duties as a baby amah in a mixture of Cantonese and Malay:

Jaga [looking after] children was *senang* [easy]. There was no need to do other work. I looked after him, bathed him and dressed him. I did not even have to wash the clothes. I just had to tidy his bed. Besides playing with him, I had to take him for a morning walk and after the walk I gave him a bath. He would then have his lunch and after lunch, I played with him again. When he was a little older, there was no need to feed him as he could do it himself. I slept in the same room. He had his own bed, I had mine.

While the baby amah was the most public of the amahs, the cook was usually the best paid and upon whom the household pivoted. The expertise of many cooks was such that most mistresses had little to do other than inform their cooks about the menus they wanted. Phyllis Tan gives an illuminating account of a typical set of weekly instructions her mother would have given to Ah Peng, the cook:

1. Today for lunch, prepare a nice soup and fried noodles for the girls.
2. *Towkah* [master] and I are not having dinner tonight.
3. Mahjong this Sunday. Please prepare *Gado-gado* [an Indonesian dish], the crab cutlet in their shells you do so well and a chicken dish and don't forget to fry the *kerupuk* [shrimp crackers]. For tea, I'll make *pulut serikaya* [a Nonya cake made with glutinous rice]. Please *pileh* [sort out the gritty grains] the *pulut* [glutinous rice] for me and soak it in water on Friday night. And can you make *Ipoh-ipoh* [a Nonya dish] for tea as well.
4. *Yee Ku-Niong*'s [second daughter] friends are coming to swim next week-end. Please prepare chicken curry and buy six loaves of French bread and cook some rice as well. For tea, *Mee-siam* [Malay-style fried noodles] and I'll bake a cake or two.
5. Uncle So-and-So or Auntie So-and-So and family are coming for dinner on Tuesday. Please cook their favourite dish.
6. Saturday lunch. *Tai Ku-Niong* [eldest daughter] and family will be coming. What about cooking *Mee Rebus* [Malay-style boiled noodles]? No? Two of the grandchildren do not have a palate for hot stuff and the youngest grandson loves *Indian Rojak* [Indian dish]. (My mother and Ah Peng agree on *Indian Rojak*.)

The instructions given to Ah Peng indicate the wide range of food she had to prepare as well as a familiarity with the preferences of various family friends and relations. She knew all the members of the extended family so well that 'not only did she know what everyone liked, she even knew how much each one ate. She was such a good judge that there was seldom any food left over. She always made sure that she satisfied everyone.' This expertise together with a sense of thrift was by no means unique. Ah Foon, the last cook the author's mother employed, displayed similar virtues. 'She was a marvellous cook. If we were going to throw a dinner party, all I had to do was to inform her of the number of people coming and the type of food required and she would do the rest. She cooked both Eastern and Western food equally well.'

Part of the cook's responsibilities was to do the marketing—a daily activity, including Sundays. Kwan Ah Sap recalls her work with an English family: 'Sometimes they gave me fixed amounts to spend. At other times, I'd pay first and settle later. If food was ordered from a grocer, I'd place an order with him and he would send her a bill at the end of the month.' It must be said that although the amahs were scrupulously honest, there was a widely accepted practice known as *ta foo tau*. This was a small financial perk the cook had when she did the marketing. Evelyn Barron elaborates: 'I gave Yeock Ha a certain amount of money and if she could make a profit on the shopping, then it was understood (though never actually discussed) that the extra cash belonged to her.' It was not always profit, however. Leong Ah Pat explains,

They gave me money for the marketing and transport. I was sometimes able to *ta foo tau*. If I bought cheaply and well, I would have some money left over, which I kept. This way, I could make a little extra. It wasn't much, only a few tens of cents, but if you bought badly, you would end up making nothing.

Most were extraordinarily thrifty. They would either walk to the nearest market to do the shopping or use the cheapest form of transport, usually a bus. The author's mother remembers:

Ah Foon would never take a taxi or even a trishaw [three-wheeled form of pedalled transport] back from the market, even when she was fully laden. She always took a bus, saying that it was a waste of money to take either a taxi or trishaw. Whatever money she was given to spend was always accounted for—to the very last cent.

In later years, when they were older and if their employer had a chauffeur, they would be taken to and from market by car.

Their thriftiness also manifested itself in a dislike of waste— probably a result of the earlier years of hardship and poverty in China when nothing was ever wasted. Sylvia Yap reveals, 'Ah

36 Marketing in Chinatown.
The cook was responsible for the marketing; she was always fastidious
about what she bought and for the lowest possible price.
(Photograph Yip Chong Fun)

Chung is very thrifty, never wanting to throw away anything that is edible. She'll reheat the left-overs until I have to fight with her to throw them away!' Or, as expressed by Ho Ah Yuet, 'It's a sin to waste anything, especially food.'

Perhaps the only drawback for amahs working as cooks for Chinese families was the Chinese custom of hospitality, which involved inviting visitors to stay for meals. Kwan Ah Sap ruefully recalls:

The Chinese keep telling you to do all sorts of things. Frequently, they'd ask friends to stay for meals even when there was not enough food. "Stay and eat, stay and eat," they would say to their friends and I would have to rummage in the refrigerator for more food to cook. In times of desperation, I fried eggs. They tend to make you do anything, regardless of time or your specific function.

She concedes, though, that it was not a bad job being a cook— 'better than being a *ta chup*'. Leong Ah Pat supports this view: 'The simplest job was being a cook. All I had to do was to cook three meals, clean up and do a few jobs like sweeping and all my work was done.' Nevertheless, she would still have to get up at around five or six each day to prepare the family breakfast, clean up after breakfast, and then do the marketing. On her return, she would have to prepare lunch. Should she be only employed as a cook, she would perhaps have some free time in the afternoon. It would then be time to prepare dinner, the main meal of the day, and around nine, after dinner was finished, the crockery, cutlery, and cooking utensils cleaned and put away and the kitchen tidied and swept. As families in the East have a tendency to entertain more often than their Western counterparts, she would be regularly involved with extra work. Sarah Chin concurs, 'When my parents gave dinner parties, and they were frequent in the 1960s, their day would perhaps end at midnight instead of at ten.'

A two-servant household with children would have a baby amah and a cook, with the housework shared between them. A typical division of labour would be for one servant to be responsible for the children as well as washing and ironing, serving the food and attending to visitors, and the cleaning and sweeping of one floor (of a two-storey house) while the other servant did the cooking and marketing together with the cleaning and sweeping of the ground floor. Should the dwelling be on a single floor or on more than two floors, the housework would be shared accordingly between them. If there were no children or if they were older and did not need looking after, a two-servant household would comprise a household maid to do all the housework and laundry, and a cook to do the cooking and marketing.

This division of labour was far more clear-cut in Hong Kong than in either Malaya or Singapore. According to Kwan Ah Sap, 'The main difference between working in Hong Kong and working in Singapore was that in Hong Kong, the jobs were well defined. You were not expected to do things not connected with your own job. Like when I cleaned, that was all I did.' In Singapore and Malaya, there was usually no precise division of labour. Often one amah would help the other out. Phyllis Tan recalls an amusing snippet: 'Ah Peng and Ah Yee worked and co-operated so well with each other, that either one, within hearing distance, would answer when called by my mother, like fetching a drink for a guest, so much so that most of our friends and relatives could not differentiate one from the other!' This co-operation was also displayed during special occasions.

A few weeks before Chinese New Year, they carried out the annual spring cleaning without direction from my mother. They also washed the window curtains and cushion covers and replaced them with the alternate set. Ah Peng would know what usual Peranakan dishes to cook. Together with Ah Yee, she knew how to lay the table in expectation of the hoards of New Year visitors. A busy first and second day for them, washing cups, plates and tumblers—all day.

They also knew what to do when, for example, the painters were sent for. All they needed to be told was "The painters are coming on Monday," and they knew exactly what to do without supervision. They would get old newspapers to cover the furniture, prepare coffee and biscuits for the painters and generally supervise them.

More typical, though, is how they worked together on the day-to-day running of the household. Lim Kian Leng remembers their routine well, having stayed at his grandmother's house on many occasions.

Ah Peng did the cooking and the marketing and also helped with the housework on Mondays. Ah Yee did the washing and ironing, the housework, served the food and helped with the washing-up. Both of them, however, actually worked as a team, each helping the other out whenever necessary.

Their day started at around 5 a.m. Ah Peng would prepare the breakfast while Ah Yee laid the table and generally tidied up. By the time we came down for breakfast, everything would be spick and span. After breakfast, Ah Peng would walk to market to do her shopping. On her return, she would check the weight of food she had bought with her own *dacing* [traditional Chinese hand-held scales] to make sure that she hadn't been cheated, and if what she bought was underweight, she would go back to the market to have it remedied!

While she was doing the marketing, Ah Yee would do the housework. She tidied the bedrooms only if there was no one present, after which she did the bathroom. They had their routine. On Monday, they cleaned the house. Both of them did it together. They moved all the furniture out of the room, if it was possible, to ensure that the cleaning was thorough. They mopped the floors (most floors were washable non-carpeted surfaces) and cleaned all the windows, standing on the sills to do it properly. They were very meticulous. Saturday was "silver-cleaning" day, when they cleaned all the cutlery and silver in the house.

These, then, were the everyday working lives of the amahs. While many of these accounts may seem quite extraordinary by present-day standards, they were typical of both the quality as well as the kind of work done by the amahs; the rule rather than the exception. Accounts such as these will, however, be familiar to most families who employed them. They help to explain why the amahs were so highly regarded and what much of their legendary reputation was based on.

37 Three *chi mui* in their *coolie fong*.
'Sisters' in life and in retirement.
(Photograph the author)

10

PRIVATE LIVES

AT the very heart of the amahs' life abroad were their sororities or sisterhoods. These provided structure and stability and evolved from their earlier days spent together in the Women's Houses in China. The importance of those experiences should not be underestimated.

There were two basic forms of sisterhood, one called the *Kit Paai Chi Mui* or Sworn-sisters Group and the other, the *Sup Chi Mui* or Ten-sister Group. The first comprised a group of unmarried girls or women who, at a formal ceremony, would pledge to help each other in all ways during their lifetime, as if they were natural sisters. The second was comparatively informal. A girl or woman wishing to join would be introduced to the rest of the group by a member (usually a relative or friend) and should she be accepted, became a member immediately. There were no other formalities. The number 'ten', in practice, was of no particular significance as any number of them could form themselves into a 'sister' group. Most amahs generally considered both as 'sworn-sister' groups and a 'sworn-sister' was referred to as a *chi mui*. In later years, all formalities were dispensed with; good friends simply regarded each other as *chi mui* or 'sisters'.

For women emigrants, these groups were essential. They provided support for single women without family. The *coolie fong* to which they would be taken on arrival was, to all intents and purposes, equivalent to the Women's Houses in China—the only difference here was that they often had to share the dwelling with others. None the less, they would be in familiar territory again. Like the *nui yan uk*, it was home—somewhere to keep their belongings, a place to return to when they were not working, and where they could be with their own kind. Without this supportive structure of 'sister' groups, life would have been extraordinarily difficult for them. With it, life was not only bearable but they were also able to enjoy a degree of freedom denied them at home.

Employment was essential to the survival of the amahs and their families in China. Fortunately, prospects in domestic service were good, albeit not very well paid. Hence, the need to supplement their income was always present. There were several ways in which they managed to add to their earnings. Tips received from helping out with extra household functions was common. Dorothy Chang remembers:

It was fairly usual for guests to tip the servants, especially if there had been a large party or they had stayed longer than overnight. On a couple of occasions, my mother made up for a guest's oversight by passing on an ostensible tip. This guest was someone my mother disliked and she knew Ah Fong cordially detested as he was unreasonable and demanding. His meanness was well known; I don't think Ah Fong was fooled but she accepted it to give my mother "face"!

Tips were also received from successful players at mahjong sessions. When parties were held, the employers would provide the tips. These were shared equally between the servants who helped. Tips left by dinner guests was a practice more prevalent in Hong Kong than in Singapore or Malaya.

A few added to their income by performing religious rites at temples or through personal winnings at games like mahjong or *tin kau*. Many invested in a tontine—an ingenious financial scheme but, being an informal arrangement based entirely on trust, it was always open to abuse. Consequently, amahs who put their money in a tontine were sometimes swindled out of their hard-earned savings by unscrupulous participants of the scheme. These abuses, plus the fact that tontines took away a sizeable amount of business from financial institutions like banks, led them eventually to be banned.

Others invested in various types of shops, preferring those run by fellow Cantonese, such as sundry-goods stores and goldsmith- or pawn-shops, from which they received interest. Banks and the Post Office were hardly ever used. The practice of *ta foo tau*, making money through the marketing, has been discussed in a previous chapter.

The most regular form of extra income received was the traditional 'red packet', known literally as *hong pau* in Singapore and Malaya and *lai see* (lucky money) in Hong Kong, received at the Chinese New Year. The amount often depended on the degree of financial success enjoyed by her employer during the previous year—anything from a few dollars to the equivalent of a month's salary. In Tang Ah Thye's experience, 'At Chinese New Year, a *hong pau* of about $20 was given. When friends of the family came, they also gave me a *hong pau*. After I had worked for six years, they gave me a $40 *hong pau*. At that stage my pay was around $200 plus. Normally *hong pau* increments went up by $20 each time.' The practice in Sarah Chin's household was not only to give an extra month's salary but also to give jewellery. 'Every Chinese New Year, my mother gave them something in 22 kt. gold, a ring or a chain. It was intended as an investment for them. They accumulated all the pieces and sold them eventually, I think, in the 1970s. The usual *hong pau* of a month's salary at New Year was also given.' This degree of generosity, although unusual, was not unique. More common was a gift of clothing or material together with the customary 'red packet'.

Most would also receive a gratuity when they left their employer's service or when they retired. Some employers actively encouraged their servants to save. Joan Oliphant said, 'My husband matched whatever they put into a joint savings account which I ran for them. Ah Choi would put in about HK$100 a month. The last we heard was that she managed to save enough to buy a flat in Hong Kong.' Only a very few, however, managed this.

The amahs were extraordinarily thrifty. Apart from the occasional jade or gold jewellery which they bought as a form of investment, their expenditure was modest, with money spent only on essential items such as food (if this was not provided), travel, personal items such as hair oil, powder, clothing and footwear, and materials for sewing and embroidery. Other expenses included rental of their *coolie fong* and the purchase of joss-sticks and other items connected with their religious activities. Many made regular payments, usually monthly, but sometimes annually, to benevolent or clan associations for 'death benefits', i.e. for the payment of their funeral expenses—the greater the amount, the grander the funeral.

Most expensive were the trips to and from China and the cost of a place in a Vegetarian House when they retired. Although personally thrifty, they were usually very generous to close friends and relatives on special occasions such as marriage. Devotion to the families they served meant that this generosity often extended to their employer's children, particularly the girls, who would be given expensive items of jewellery in jade or gold on events such as birth, marriage, and on going abroad to study. Brides of sons in the family would also be presented with a gift. The traditional 'red packet' at Chinese New Year was always given to their employer's unmarried children and grandchildren (if any). All these gifts were, in effect, from a mother/grandmother to her children/ grandchildren. Even European children were not excluded. Cyrena Tinker recalls, 'Ah Fong gave us little red envelopes with money in them every Chinese New Year.'

Remittances were their most tangible link with China and upon them the survival of many families in China depended. Virtually every amah sent money home, although the amounts as well as the frequency varied. During times of full employment, it was estimated that approximately 20 per cent of their wages was spent on normal items, 10 per cent on subscriptions, and 70 per cent was saved or remitted. In the 1950s, the height of the amah era, they sent home about $200 a year, although there were some who sent up to $500 (the average salary was $100 per month). Money tended to be sent at times coinciding with the important Chinese festivals, particularly Chinese New Year (January/February). Others were the Ching Ming Festival (All Souls' Day) (April), the Festival of the Hungry Ghosts (July), and the Mid-Autumn or Mooncake Festival (September/October). At other times, remittances were usually sent at the relatives' request.

Although remittances took a large part of their savings, many considered them as much an investment as a demonstration of filial piety. Normally, a remittance was to be utilized for a variety of purposes, unless the sender specifically requested that it be used for a particular purpose only. In general, the basic needs of food, clothing, and shelter took first priority. After these were satisfied, the money would then be used to purchase land and oxen and to build a house. This last item was often for their own use when they retired and, in return for the help they had given over the years, they would expect to be supported by their relatives on their return to China.

Several methods were used to remit money home. The most common was the use of the remittance department of banks, usually the Bank of China, as well as those of firms with contacts or branches close to the emigrants' home villages. Goldsmith shops were also popular. For a small fee, the bank or firm would remit the money to China. At the other end, an employee of the receiving bank or firm would go to the emigrants' villages and hand over the remittances. Money was also taken back by returning relatives, 'sisters', or the *sui haak*. In all these cases, payment was either in kind or, more usually, in the form of a 'red packet'. The relative or 'sister' taking the remittance back would be given a sum of money, ostensibly for her food and not for services rendered, it being considered an insult to pay a relative or 'sister' for such a task.

Their lives were spent almost entirely within the family household other than the occasional day off. Free time during their normal workdays was usually spent attending to personal matters such as washing, brushing, and oiling the hair as well as the ingenious (though painful) process used in plucking facial hair. This last was achieved by winding thread between the fingers and using it in a scissors-like action to remove the hair. For many, favourite pastimes were sewing, embroidery, and patchwork—a result of earlier skills acquired in China, particularly in the Girls' Houses. Some, however, like Chong Yuen Cheong, only acquired their considerable skills in sewing as well as cooking 'on the job'. Titus Pawle, now living in Australia, remembers that 'Chong Yuen Cheong arrived totally untrained'. Baby amahs often made clothes for the children. Many were excellent seamstresses, able to manage even the most intricate smocking.

Their closest relationships were with their 'sisters', whom they visited on days off. Regular visits were also made to their *coolie fong* to check for mail and to have a chat with whoever was there. Dorothy Chang agrees:

Her time off was when she had nothing to do in the house. Her friends from the same *kongsi fong* worked for people we knew or who lived nearby—so there would be a lot of coming and going amongst them. Sometimes she would go into town to her *kongsi fong* but normally the visits were housecalls.

Some employers were not happy with visits, considering them distracting, but most did not mind, as long as these calls did not interfere with work. Amahs in Hong Kong tended to visit their *chi mui fong* less frequently. There was less incentive to do so as conditions there were far more cramped and uncomfortable than the *coolie fong* of their counterparts in Singapore and Malaya. Many also did not need to leave their place of employment to talk to friends. They were able to have daily conversations with other amahs across the balconies of their employers' flats. The only times when most members of a *coolie fong* met were on festival days.

38 Amahs at prayer in a cave temple in Ipoh.
Religion—essential to their moral well-being and
necessary for their spiritual survival.
(Courtesy Department of Information, Malaysia)

Live street operas, once widespread and popular with the amahs, are sadly rare nowadays, having been largely replaced by television and video recordings. The cinema, too, was very popular before the advent of television. Leong Siew Kee recalls that she did not really like going out: 'I did not often visit my *chi mui* but the cinema—ah, I enjoyed that. I would go on my days off. In the old days, some baby amahs only had one day off a month. I had one day off every two weeks, then one day off a week.' Others were not so fortunate. In Tang Ah Thye's words:

I had very little time off. I didn't go to the *wayang* (street opera) or visit *chi mui*. I didn't have many *chi mui* anyway. I never rest. Sometimes I'd take a bus to my *coolie fong* to see if I had any letters. If there were any, I would have them read by a letter writer. I would then head home and cook the next meal. Sometimes I would finish the day's work before going off.

Contact with China was maintained through occasional visits, remittances, and letters. Most amahs in the Nanyang visited China between two to four times during their life abroad. These visits were of practical as well as social importance. Jade or gold jewellery, particularly the latter, was often taken back, as well as everyday items such as lamps and even bicycles. On their return, they always brought back something for the families they worked for, especially the children. The amahs in Hong Kong returned to China frequently, at least once a year; Chinese New Year was an especially popular time for visits. Many also went during Ching Ming to pay their respects at ancestral graves.

With the passing of time, both remittances and letters dwindled due mainly to the death of close relatives. By the time they retired, most of the surviving relatives were usually nieces or nephews and their families. Letters home normally contained the usual enquiries about health and family matters. Mention would also be made about their successful life-style abroad, true or otherwise—to give them 'face', it being important to do well. If excessive requests for money were made, however, they usually resorted to writing about their own difficulties abroad. Letters from China were invariably about the hardships there, how the family was doing, and often ended with further requests for money.

As virtually all the amahs were illiterate, the services of a letter-writer, found in all densely populated Chinese areas, were indispensable. His 'premises'—usually set up on the pavement—comprised a small portable table and the paraphernalia of his trade:

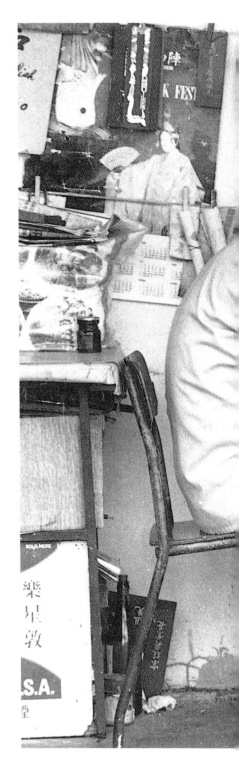

39　A letter-writer.
He was an essential link with home for the illiterate amahs.
(Photograph the author)

paper, brushes, pens, ink, and envelopes, and stools for his customers. Samples of his work would adorn any spare adjacent wall space. His fee for writing letters was modest. In the 1950s, depending on length, charges ranged from 50 cents to $1. Regular customers would have mail read free. Others would pay a small sum—about 20 cents—for this service. He also wrote signs and anything else requiring his calligraphic skills. Increasing literacy has meant that his services are less needed in the 1980s and only a few still remain.

Most amahs believed in a mixture of ancestor-worship, Taoism, and Buddhism. Temples were regularly visited for offerings to be made and there was always an altar at their *coolie fong* and in their quarters at their employers' residences. Although they were not all vegetarians, most would have a completely vegetarian diet (cooked in separate pots and pans) twice a month, usually on the first and fifteenth days. Despite any profundity of belief, their religion served to underpin their lives, giving it purpose and structure. While 'sister' groups were an essential feature of everyday life, religion was intrinsic to their moral well-being and provided them with the necessary spiritual strength for survival abroad.

An essential facet of Chinese tradition and religion is the belief in what is termed 'fate'—the acceptance of one's lot in life. But this belief, while essential to the amahs' survival, also restricted their aspirations. Many looked uncomprehending when asked about their aims in life. With the hardship and rigidity of life in China, especially where women were concerned, simply to survive was enough. Achievement of any sort of independent life-style was probably more than they could have hoped for. The fact that all the amahs attained a high degree of independence abroad meant that they had effectively fulfilled their aspirations in life, albeit unstated. To consciously think about other aims and ambitions was a luxury seldom indulged in.

The few aspirations that were actually mentioned were simple. Tang Ah Thye echoed the wish of some—a wistful desire for literacy: 'I would have liked to have been able to read and write as I would not have to rely on a letter-writer and I would be able to find my way around and read road signs, notices, etc.' Leong Ah Pat voiced the aims of most when she said, 'I would like to remain independent and not have to rely on others.'

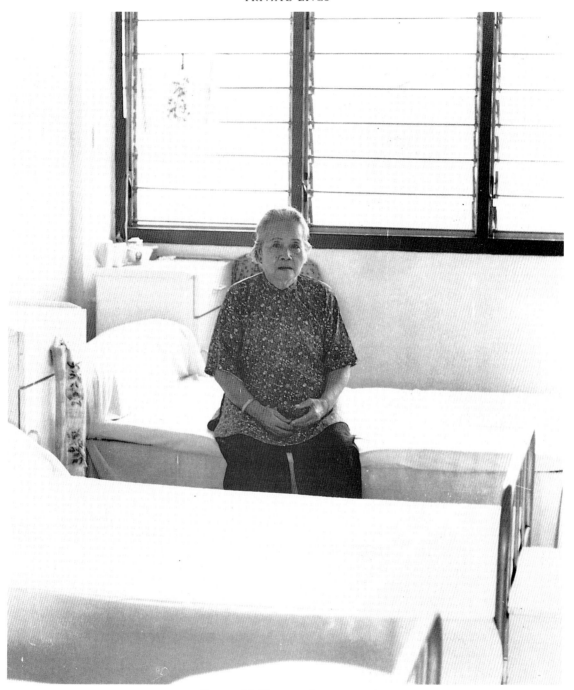

40 Leong Ah Pat, aged seventy-nine.
'I would like to remain independent and not have to rely on others.'
(Photograph the author)

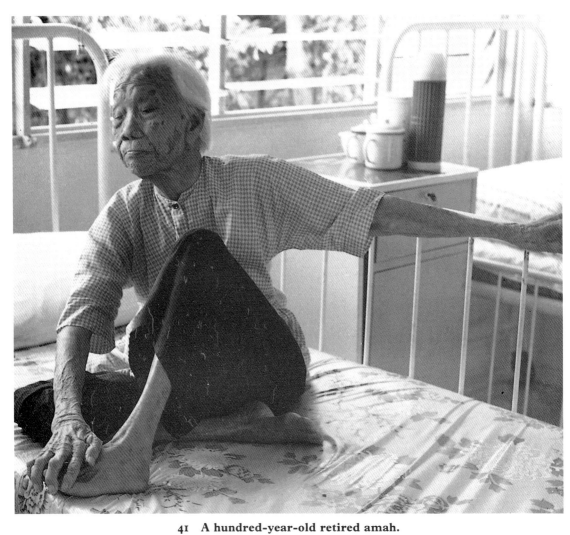

41 A hundred-year-old retired amah.
Blind and in ill-health but still indomitable.
(Photograph the author)

11

HEALTH, OLD AGE, AND
A QUICK DEATH

HEALTH was understandably the main concern of the women. Without good health, survival would have been impossible. It was usual for people in China, especially the women, to be knowledgeable about Chinese herbal cures as well as other aspects of medicine. The amahs were no exception. All were familiar with Chinese folk medicine. Ane Bangert-Cave, who lived in Penang, recalls: 'I can remember very vividly Ah See's special skill in concoctions for all sorts of ailments. She was very knowledgeable about herbal medicine.' The *ma cheh* in particular were supposed to be experts in the field, including knowing how to resuscitate new-born babies with breathing difficulties. Some *ma cheh* were even reputed to have certain magical powers due to cult practices.

Many families have cause to be grateful to the medical knowledge and skills of their amahs. Sylvia Yap says thankfully, 'When we are sick, she's always there to mother and fuss over us. She never gives up and will go round the market until she gets hold of another remedy. If she knows that we are having a stressful time, she'll always boil her famous herbal energy-giving soup to re-vitalize us.' Phyllis Tan benefited in a different way. 'Her skilled fingers would massage away sprained ankle or tennis elbow to health in no time. Although the pain was excruciating when the obstructed blood vessels were massaged, I was grateful for her healing fingers.'

Almost all the amahs were astonishingly healthy. Comments such as 'they themselves never seemed to get sick' and 'she is as strong as an ox and has never been sick' were made by many employers. Tong Yuet Ching offers a succinct explanation for this: 'Rich people usually fall ill because they don't exercise and never fully use their energy. Poor people worked all day, therefore they always exercised their muscles and bones. If you are hard-working you will not often fall ill.' Another reason was that they also took great care over their health, knowing that ill-health could mean the loss of their jobs—workers in the past did not enjoy much job security. When they occasionally fell ill, they would take the appropriate Chinese herbs or medicine. The result of all this was that, although poor, they were often much healthier than their employers. The illnesses they did succumb to were hidden ones like diabetes, high blood pressure, and cancer which, because they were uncomplaining, were often not detected until it was too late.

The practice among most local employers was that if they took their servant to the doctor, they would meet the costs, but if the servant went to the doctor herself, she would have to pay the bills. There were, of course, employers who paid for all expenses, including hospitalization. Expatriate employers often met all their amahs' medical expenses.

These women were generally suspicious of Western medicine, preferring to seek traditional Chinese remedies for minor ailments. Should treatment be necessary, they would go to a Chinese physician. If they could not afford the cost of treatment, they would go to free institutions such as the Tong Chai Medical Institution in Singapore, where 'the poor and the needy could be treated free of charge, according to Chinese medical beliefs'. If hospitalization was required, there were institutions like the Tung Wah Hospital in Hong Kong or the Kwong Wai Shiu Hospital in Singapore. Both were specifically founded to cater for the needs of the Cantonese and once were staffed only by Cantonese personnel. Patients paid what they could afford.

Many terminally ill or very elderly women, particularly those who were *sor hei*, often shunned hospitals, preferring to die in 'death houses' such as those of Sago Lane in Singapore, now no longer in existence. One reason was their suspicion of Western medical treatment and the other was the wish to be attended to by their 'sisters'; even in death, they did not want to be touched or handled by men. These macabre places held wakes and often had an undertaker on the ground floor while the ailing inmates occupied the upper floors or the rear of the building. Depressing as they were, many chose to spend their last days there rather than in a hospital. Residency here was not free. Inmates were looked after by their 'sisters', who provided both food and medicine. By common consent, amahs agreed that they should not die in their *coolie fong*. Thus, with nowhere else to go, many would end up in one of these houses. Regardless of how horrific these places were, they fulfilled a social need of the time. With these houses gone, they now rely on charitable and government institutions.

With their philosophic view of life, death was not something to be feared—only the manner of dying. Most just wanted to die quickly and 'not be a burden on others'.

Retirement was the other major concern of amahs in Singapore and Malaya as most were single and, unlike those in Hong Kong, had no family close at hand. Many amahs in Hong Kong had relatives there with whom they could live when they retired.

There was no such thing as a 'retirement age' for amahs. Most usually retired only when they were too old or too ill to work. Many worked until they were well into their seventies. It has often been said that the Chinese could do without any form of institutional help as their family system provided the most efficient kind of social insurance possible. While this may have been true of extended families in China, it did not apply to single women abroad.

Unmarried women in China could live in their father's house, but if they had taken the vows of *sor hei*, they would have to live in a Women's House on retirement. Those not in China could choose either to return or to remain abroad.

Although many were able to realize the once common ambition of returning to China to die, there were still a considerable number who chose to remain abroad for a number of different reasons: no immediate family still alive in China, their becoming accustomed to life and even the climate abroad—'no more four seasons', and having their 'sisters' around.

Some anticipated their retirement well in advance by adopting a young girl as 'old-age security', i.e. with the express purpose of having that 'adopted daughter' look after them when they retired. These were unofficial adoptions as the girls were usually given away by their parents. A 'red packet' was always presented to the mother as a token and not as payment. The giving away of daughters was practised when families were large and daughters many. Some were also given away because they had been born with an 'unlucky horoscope', i.e. one believed to bring bad luck to the parents or, in some cases, when the horoscope predicted their later unsuitability for marriage. Some 'adopted daughters' were looked after by the amahs at their place of work—dependent, of course, on the approval of their employer. Others paid families to look after their adopted daughters.

42 Effigy of an amah.
A papier-mâché effigy of a deceased amah sitting down for a feast
during the Festival of the Hungry Ghosts. With funds left behind to pay for
occasions such as these, her soul is guaranteed not to go hungry.
(Photograph the author)

The *chai tong* or Vegetarian House was the most popular choice amongst amahs. There were some exceptions, one of whom was Ah Nui. She became a Catholic convert and retired to a home run by the 'Little Sisters of the Poor' as she felt that the Catholic nuns were kinder than the women who ran the Vegetarian House. As its name suggests, a Vegetarian House was intended for women who were vegetarians. It could be owned by a Buddhist nunnery or monastery, a group of women members, or a woman on her own. Some were even built by devout Buddhist business-men. In all cases, they were run by the women themselves. The purpose of these houses was to provide board and lodging for unmarried Buddhist women and those without immediate family who had no one to care for them and nowhere else to go in their old age. The majority of these houses were formed to meet the needs of Chinese immigrant women workers.

These houses were often organized on a clan basis and even according to the districts or villages in China from which their members originally came. This was particularly true of those started by immigrant women members. Vegetarian Houses were liked as they provided security, companionship, a sense of belonging, and more freedom than found in government or charitable homes. Foong Ah Chat says simply, 'I treat it as my home.' Another important consideration for these women was the guarantee of a proper funeral with the provision of a band, mourners (fellow residents), and soul tablets being placed in the Tablet hall; in other words, a Vegetarian House provided 'care while alive and a funeral at death'.

Amahs who had planned on retiring to a Vegetarian House usually reserved a place well in advance, either by paying a lump sum or in instalments. Foong Ah Chat paid $700 some forty years ago to secure her place at the Fei Ha Ching Hsia Home. Some women chose to 'live' here instead of at a *coolie fong*. These were women who usually did not belong to a sisterhood. Should a prospective resident be able to pay the full cost of the place, she would have few (if any) duties to perform upon taking up resi-dency. The extent of her duties was inversely proportional to the amount she paid.

A woman wishing to join a Vegetarian House would select one she had heard about or where she already had friends or 'sisters' staying. She would then be introduced to and interviewed by the woman in charge. Conditions of entry, including financial terms, would be discussed and should the interview prove satisfactory,

43 The Fei Ha Ching Hsia Home.

The *chai tong*: 'I treat it as my home.'

(Photograph the author)

44 Only a few still remain.
One of the few surviving historical Chinatown buildings in Singapore
still housing the amahs' *coolie fong*.
(Photograph the author)

146

the appropriate arrangements regarding payment were made. She would then be issued with a receipt and, in some cases, be given a book certifying that she was a member of that home. If it belonged to a particular Buddhist sect, the book would also normally state her entitlement to stay at any of its homes, whether abroad or in China.

The regime in Vegetarian Houses is normally quite relaxed, the women being able to come and go freely, and to have visitors at most times. There are many similarities to the *coolie fong*. As in the *coolie fong*, they cook and eat individually—each member has her own cooker. They sleep on wooden bunks in shared rooms and store their belongings against the wall and under the bed. It is easy to see why these houses are popular with the women. They are simply a more comfortable extension of their *coolie fong* but with greater emphasis on religion; in effect, a home for women run on religious lines.

There are also homes attached to temples and run by Buddhist nuns. These are similar to the Vegetarian House but with some differences. There are usually fewer residents, and the regime is stricter, with a stronger religious content. Some, like the Tai Pei Old People's Home for elderly Chinese women in Singapore, although attached to a temple, exist as homes in their own right— a cross between the relaxed atmosphere of most Vegetarian Houses and the more regimented environment of most government or charitable institutions.

Residents here have a reasonable amount of freedom and are able to do what they like between set meal times—usually sewing, chatting, or sleeping. The more devout spend much of their time praying. As in other old-age homes, a popular pastime is the watching of video recordings of Chinese opera in the evenings. Accommodation is clean but spartan. Prospective tenants are interviewed to determine their financial status, their ability to work, and questioned generally to determine their suitability. Those felt by the nuns to be mentally or physically ill, bedridden, too aggressive, or suffering from an infectious disease would be turned away. Application for residency can be made by the women themselves, by friends already there, by relatives, or by government agencies acting on their behalf.

The chronically ill are looked after in state hospitals. For those who are acutely sick, there are government as well as charitable establishments, such as the Home for the Aged Sick in Singapore which 'provides companionship, the care and cleanliness of a

45   Retired amahs sitting on steps.
Watching the world pass them by.
(Photograph the author)

46 Retired amahs selling vegetables by the roadside.
Even in retirement, some still have to work.
(Photograph the author)

home for those who are sick and have no family to care for them or those families through their own poverty are unable to support them, and who are also too sick to look after themselves without some expert care'. This is more a residential hospital than a retirement home, with the inmates sleeping in dormitories rather than sharing rooms.

Amahs able to buy or rent a flat of their own are few and far between. Sometimes the gratuity given on retirement is large enough to enable them to purchase a house or flat of their own. Some remained with their employers until their death. The author's mother recalls:

Ah Foon worked for us from 1955 till the day she died in 1975. She had expressed a wish that she wanted to die in our household, which we respected. After her death, per her wishes, we sold all her jewellery and remitted the proceeds to her nephew in China. As she had not made any provision for her funeral, we took care of the arrangements which we knew she wanted.

There are still, however, some who continue to live in their *coolie fong*, despite the primitive conditions, due to a combination of several factors—desire for continued independence, lack of funds to move elsewhere, or a preference to remain with the familiar. Some supplement their meagre funds by selling vegetables, fruit or small-goods by the roadside in Chinatown. For others, the only escape from their dingy quarters is to sit in public spaces, spending the time in conversation and watching the world pass them by.

Even though one can admire their dogged determination in wishing to remain independent, it is hard not to feel a sense of sadness seeing them still having to work at eighty, sitting on public steps, or languishing in their *coolie fong*. Sarah Chin expresses a sentiment shared by many: 'They worked and cared for others all their lives and saw their own families so infrequently that there was no hope for a life of their own, a home or a family. It is sad that for so many of them, there is no one to care for them when they grow old.'

47   Tong Yuet Ching, aged eighty-three.
'I don't owe anybody anything.'
(Photograph the author)

12

A MOST REMARKABLE LADY

TONG YUET CHING embodies all that is special about Cantonese amahs: independent, hard-working, and indomitable. She is illiterate, comes from an agricultural background, and worked as an amah for almost fifty years. Her experiences and the views she holds are similar to those of other amahs but her exceptional clarity of expression is not. Her philosophy of life is simple, uncompromising, and direct—a lesson for all. As her views typify those held by most amahs, the following selection provides an invaluable insight into these remarkable women. She remains, at eighty-three, an extraordinary woman among extraordinary women.

Life: Man's life is so short. What is there to be sad about? So why not spend your mind on your job? When there is food to eat, you eat. This is my way of life.

Attitude to Others: The most important thing of all is to have a kind and compassionate heart.

Bringing up Children: You should see what he wants. Protect him from the cold and feed him punctually. He must be kept clean and do not frighten him. You should not shout at a baby as a baby is very delicate.

You should not hit children. A girl I looked after was four when her father hit her for not eating her food. She said that it made her very angry then. She is eighteen now but she has not forgotten. Hitting is not a good method of teaching a child.

To get a child to do what you want, you should talk to him in a gentle voice. Wait until he is free, then ask him to do it for you. There are some who will ask you to wait but then go out to play. Children are like that. Wait till he comes back and ask him again, until he does it for you. And if there are breakable things, put them out of reach.

Wealth: No good, because no matter how much you want, how much you get, you will never be able to bring it to the coffin. I do not know

153

whether I would be happier or not if I were rich. I am not in a position to tell. I have never experienced being rich.

Aspirations: Would I like to have been educated? There is no point thinking about what I would have wanted or not wanted. Should the chance arise, then I'll think of it. I have no ambitions, except to have work, good health and to die fast.

Work: If you work for long, your boss would be able to see for himself whether you can be trusted or not. If you pretend, you can only pretend for a short time—not for long. He has eyes to see for himself whether you are any good or not.

I would not complain if I was given extra work. I [have] maintained this attitude all my life. If you draw a salary and have taken the job willingly, then you should do your job properly because it is your responsibility. If you are not happy, you can always resign.

I always did my job absolutely well and so if my bosses complained, I would always answer them back. After I explained to them exactly what I had done, they would nod their heads.

Death: I am not afraid of death. We definitely have to die one day. Even emperors have to die; what's more, I am only an ant. Therefore, I do not fear death. I would like to fall ill for two or three days, then pass away. I do not wish to be a burden on others.

Funerals: Funeral services are a waste of money. How would the dead know? Funeral processions are only for the living to watch.

Christianity: A Christian sister came to see me and told me, "Believe in Jesus and you shall go to Heaven and if you don't, you shall go to Hell." I can't believe it. Has anyone been there?

Buddhism: Buddhist nuns and priests are the same as any normal human beings. Nothing special.

Envy: I do not envy others. People who are beautiful are just born like that. If they are richer than we are, that is their fate, so why envy them?

Independence: It is good not to have to rely on others. I have never borrowed even five cents from anyone. If I have more money, I would spend more. If not, I would be more thrifty. I don't bother people and I don't owe anybody anything.

48 Most important of all.
'...to have a kind and compassionate heart.'
(Photograph the author)

49 Elegant and immaculate.
A devoted, caring amah—although perhaps not appreciated in this case!
(Courtesy Joanna Wormald)

13

'WE WERE VERY LUCKY TO HAVE THEM'

LIVE-IN domestic servants occupy a special position in employer-employee relations. Continual contact between employer and servant can breed familiarity. Although this taking-for-granted type of relationship can lead to exploitation, it can also create a bond going far beyond the accepted norm. With few exceptions, all employers thought highly of their amahs and considered them 'loyal, hard-working, reliable and honest'.

The Chinese and the expatriates were the largest groups of employers. The British formed the vast majority of this latter group, as they were present in substantial numbers in business, the civil service, and the armed forces until the late 1960s. If there was a basic difference in attitude between these two groups, it would have been a tendency for Chinese families to take their amahs for granted while the British would have valued them more highly. This was probably due to the fact that while servants were an established feature of middle-class life in the Far East, they were not commonplace in Britain. There were, of course, wide differences in attitude between individual employers, both expatriate and Chinese.

With servants readily at hand, few middle-class wives, either local or expatriate, ever did any of the household chores. This was especially appreciated by the European women, who were able to enjoy an unprecedented array of social activities such as morning and afternoon tea, lunches, dinners, bridge clubs, and parties.

The key figure in households with children was the baby amah. Most were highly thought of and devoted to the children in their care. Betty Wardle, whose husband was Chaplain of the Missions to Seamen in Singapore, lived there before the Second World War. She recalls:

Lau Ah Moi was a dedicated and responsible baby amah. She came into hospital with me when both my daughters were born and took charge of them from the first. She kept to a good steady routine—always with the care and comfort of the children foremost in her mind. She had a great sense of humour and became very fond of the children, and we, of her.

Many of the children were equally devoted to their amahs. Joan Oliphant remembers how unhappy her ten-year-old daughter was when they were about to leave Hong Kong. 'I asked her what the matter was, thinking perhaps that she was simply upset at leaving. She replied, "Mummy, you don't understand. I have two mothers and I have to leave one of them." Ah Choi and her were on that level, very close.' Cyrena Tinker, now twenty-seven, recalls that Ah Fong, the baby amah, was 'very proud of all three of us and fiercely protective. She was especially fond of Celia, the youngest, and treated her like her own baby and fed her Chinese food and took her to visit her friends.' This possessive attitude was not uncommon among baby amahs and although appreciated by many, some found it too obsessive and felt that it 'undermined the natural bond between mother and child'.

There was also a difference in attitude between the British who were there for a fixed period, e.g. military personnel or businessmen, and the long-stay colonials. The ones who did not stay long usually regarded their servants as a luxurious novelty. Confesses Evelyn Barron, 'I tended to treat the whole situation as a lovely bonus to my overseas life, which I would remember with nostalgia when I was back home being an ordinary mum.' She also recalls that 'the position and attitude of the servants towards army personnel depended very much on the rank of the husband. Officers' families tended to be more aloof with their amahs than did the Other Ranks' families who tended to treat them more like an English "daily" [i.e. in a friendly manner; a "daily" was a woman who came each day to do the housework]. The amahs reciprocated in like manner.'

The very nature of their existence abroad—single women without families—made the majority of them totally devoted employees. The Chinese family is an intricate and powerful social unit with clear-cut roles for every member. Although individually limiting, it provided a secure framework for most. This cushioning structure, for the vast majority of amahs, however, did not exist. Without a family to depend on or to care for, they had to fend for themselves and transferred emotions and loyalties normally reserved for their own families, to those of their employers. Wan Yong Gui explains why. She worked for the Ong family for some fifty years till she retired. Her response is typical:

I liked the family and their relatives. They all treated me well. They didn't look down on me—[they were] like my own people. So why change jobs? Even now that I am retired, he [the son she first looked after in the 1930s] still treats me well. He is very respectful and helps me whenever I need help.

Many employers greatly valued their sense of devotion to the family. Dorothy Chang remembers:

Just after we moved to Kuala Lumpur, the health of my maternal grandmother deteriorated rapidly and we couldn't get any nurses to stay. Ah Fong willingly helped my mother to nurse her. As she was both incontinent and spent the last four days in a coma, this was not a pleasant task, but Ah Fong said that it wouldn't be right to put her in a hospital so close to the end.

While some employers undoubtedly exploited this sense of loyalty, others were deeply appreciative and treated them 'like an aged and respected relative'. She recalls an earlier incident, when, as a girl, she was cheeky to the servant:

My grandmother overheard this and that evening when my parents came home, she informed them of my rudeness to the servant and all hell broke loose. I was raked over the coals and was told in no uncertain terms that I was not to speak like that to anybody, especially a servant, as she could not answer back.

Sarah Chin was told by her mother that she was never to refer to their baby amah, Lee Ah Thai, as her 'servant' but by the honorific term, *cheh* (older sister). She recalls her childhood relationship with Ah Thai with much affection: 'In company and in the presence of my parents, she was duly respectful, but alone together, we were friends. She decided what was best and I obeyed—most of the time!' The high regard in which some families held their servants is illustrated by the following anecdote, when her mother took it upon herself to teach their servants to read and write Chinese. Most amahs were completely illiterate.

My mother taught our amahs to read and write over twenty years ago. I remember that we [the children] sat down for lessons with the three of them every fortnight. She taught them how to hold a pen as they had never held one in their lives. They wrote their names first of all and did this for months on end. She taught them for many, many years. Sometimes the lessons were dreadful and she would shout at them in exasperation, "You're so stupid!" And they would laugh and laugh and go away to practise. In the end, they learned and could read a Chinese newspaper. It was wonderful!

The reputation that all amahs were wonderful was not always true. P. G. Lim recalls just such a one in her early days in Penang:

'Not all amahs were the models that they were made out to be. Some were tyrants in the household in which they resided. We had one in our household of five servants.' Some employers felt that 'if they respected you and vice-versa, they would give their life for you. If not, they would be contrary.' If there was any fault of the amahs singled out by employers, it was usually their 'bossiness', but even this was really about pride in their work and their sense of professionalism. Evelyn Barron reveals,

One drawback was that if I wanted to make myself an occasional coffee or tea, I did not dare venture into the kitchen unless she [the amah] was off for the day. She considered it to be an impertinence and if I wanted something, it would be brought in on a tray complete with tray cloth, etc.

She concedes, however, that 'it was a small price to pay for the luxury of having such a willing servant'. But regardless of any faults they had, including a lack of expertise, the most valued quality was undoubtedly the amahs' sense of loyalty, as in the case of Eva Lo's servant, Chan Yin-Fong. 'She did not do well in any type of work, nor could she cook. She was not too intelligent. But she was loyal.' She was so devoted to the family that once, during the occupation of Hong Kong in the Second World War, she voluntarily took the place of her mistress whom the Japanese had come to arrest. Fortunately, the alleged offence was a minor one and she was bailed out in the morning.

Stories abound of their loyalty to their employers. One concerns an English doctor who had taken his amah back to England to look after his child. On the return trip to Malaya, the child fell overboard and the amah jumped into the ocean after him. Both were drowned. Another is about an amah travelling from China to Singapore with two children in her care. One night, there was a terrible storm which tossed the ship about. In the morning, she was found sitting on one of the bunks, tightly clutching a child under each arm—with a broken leg. It had been broken during the course of the storm and despite the agony, she spent all night protecting and comforting the children as best she could, rather than draw attention to herself. There were also instances of amahs in Singapore going out to work to support employers who had lost their jobs during the Second World War. Lee Ah Lian worked for a Bengali employer and when he 'went broke', she stayed loyally with the family and worked for a year without pay, rather than seek a job elsewhere.

50 Loyal, hard-working, reliable, and honest.
A common appreciation and they were also often
regarded as a member of the family.
(Courtesy M. Namazie)

Dorothy Chang voices sentiments many families felt about their long-serving amahs:

I find it difficult to assess Ah Fong's position in the household. I took her position so much for granted. She could be annoying and sometimes infuriating but she was always there. In many ways, I feel a virtual sense of bereavement that she is no longer with us (she returned to China) and knowing that it is most unlikely that I shall ever see her again. I miss her more than I missed either of my grandmothers when they died.

Sarah Chin expresses a simple appreciation: 'We loved all three of them. They were kind, treated us as their children and had end-less patience and incredible humility. They were honest beyond description.'

Although the employer was the husband/father, their relation-ship was invariably with the mother/wife and the children. Dorothy Chang says, 'As far as my mother was concerned, Ah Fong was a friend and a confidante. I think this feeling was mutual.' Chan Poh Yee, now living in Canada, had a similar view: 'Ah Hoy was a very caring person and devoted to me and my baby son. I considered her both a member of the family and a friend.'

Not only did they become part of everyday family life, they also shared in the family's joys and sorrows. 'When my grandfather died, Ah Peng and Ah Yee attended the funeral as members of the family—not as servants,' recalls Lim Kian Leng.

Perhaps the high regard and affection in which the amahs were held by Chinese families is best expressed by Sylvia Yap, while Joan Oliphant offers the expatriate view:

Our amah, Ah Chung, has been with our family for thirty-three years. She was originally employed as a baby amah. She now does the cooking and housework. We all treat her as a member of the family. She's like a grandmother to us and treats us like her grandchildren. She is very dedicated, hard-working and caring. Like all 'black and whites', she nags, but viewing it positively, I think that this is the best proof that she cares and although sometimes irritating, I must admit that all her nagging is related to my well-being. We would like her to stay with us when she has retired. (Sylvia Yap.)

We adored both Ah Siew and Ah Choi and always considered them friends who helped me with the children. We did not exploit them. We respected them as people. They were not just servants to be ordered about. Both of them displayed total devotion to us. There was great love for their charges (both were baby amahs). It was not an employee/employer relationship—much more than that. They were very proud and very professional. They had enormous integrity, loyalty and respect. We were very lucky to have them. (Joan Oliphant.)

**51 Tang Ah Thye, aged seventy-five,
and Leong Siew Kee, aged seventy-nine.**

'We were very lucky to have them.'
(Photograph the author)

52 Chin Ah Ooi, still working at seventy-three.
'Superior servants. . . .'
(Photograph the author)

14

SUPERIOR SERVANTS;
EXTRAORDINARY WOMEN

THE 'youngest' of the amahs interviewed still working, Lui Wai
Foon, was born in 1918, which makes her seventy in 1988, an age
when most people would already have been retired for at least five
years. The majority of Cantonese women who came to work as
amahs arrived in the 1930s and are now in their seventies, some
in their eighties.

Due to immigration restrictions in Singapore and Malaya,
though not Hong Kong, and changing conditions after the Second
World War, the number of Cantonese women leaving the Pearl
River Delta to enter domestic service began to decrease. With
the advent of the factory age, many young women now preferred
working in factories with set working conditions rather than
being tied to a job they regarded as domestic drudgery. With new
job opportunities available as well as increased social awareness,
there was a marked change in attitude to domestic service. The
subservient position of the domestic servant became increasingly
less acceptable. Education played a crucial part not only in in-
creasing literacy but also in extending the horizons of the women.
They became more selective as a result. Many eschewed what
they saw as the lowly status of servants and many who might previously have gone into domestic service now no longer did so.
The irony was that, with more wives going to work, there was,
for the first time, a genuine need for household servants as dis-
tinct from the social demands of the past.

The departure of the British in the late 1960s left many amahs
in search of employment. Fortunately, due to the increased
demand for servants among the local population, jobs were easy
to obtain, though not perhaps with the conditions of service they
had enjoyed under the British. None the less, most were able to
command better wages and secure improved working conditions.

By the 1970s, with many amahs retiring or returning to China and their numbers not being replaced, the age of the Cantonese amah began drawing to a close. Their places were taken by a succession of women of different races, culminating in the ubiquitous Filipinas, none of whom have come even remotely close to offering the same quality of service or commitment. When the few Cantonese amahs still in employment are gone, this unique group of women will be no more.

Although unique, were they exceptional or simply exploited? On the face of it, the amahs, with their low wages and poor conditions of work, bear all the characteristics of exploited labour. And although few employers deliberately exploited them, most would appear to have taken advantage of the amahs' sense of professionalism and loyalty. On this basis, it would be true to say that they were exploited. Harder to understand, though, is why these women should have shown such expertise and devotion— qualities hardly characteristic of the exploited. And they were women of considerable independence and character as well.

In the 1930s, when most of them arrived, there was a variety of jobs available to illiterate, unskilled women in labouring, agriculture, hawking and, of course, domestic service. Work was also available in shops and factories. There was no shortage of jobs; in fact, plantation and mine owners were so desperate for labour that they sent their agents to Kwangtung to recruit women workers. Neither were they ignorant of pay and conditions. Most already had friends and relatives abroad and it was not unusual for the women to set levels of pay themselves. It would appear odd that they should choose not only to become amahs but also were content to remain as such for the rest of their working lives.

Although independent and enterprising, they were restricted by the simple fact that they were Chinese women—brought up in a traditional and highly structured society which considered them inferior. Confucian teachings emphasized the inferiority of women to men and defined the importance of filial piety while Buddhism and Taoism, among other things, taught them to accept their destiny—'It is our fate.' Part of this acceptance was to regard marriage and dependency on men as essential and inevitable. While most of China accepted this, the Cantonese women of the Pearl River Delta did not. Their vows of celibacy, sisterhoods, and Women's Houses all attest to this. But while they were able to break with tradition and achieve social and economic independence, they were, nevertheless, still so conditioned regarding their inferior status that they also accepted whatever happened to them in life. Most amahs had no ambitions other than those connected with maintaining their independence and the desire to return to China one day.

They chose domestic service because, in comparison with their lives in China, it was easy. It was thus not surprising that despite the poor pay and conditions, there were few complaints. And what should not be forgotten is that, regardless of the difficulties domestic service posed, it was still infinitely preferable to the life they would have led had they chosen marriage. As wives in China, they would have had no freedom of any kind, neither social nor economic, and they would have had to bear ill-treatment by the in-laws as well. Consequently, they were considerably better off as servants than they would have been as wives.

Their expertise, diligence, honesty, and devotion were grounded in their earlier lives in China where such qualities were ordinary aspects of everyday life. Suggests Leong Hock Kam, 'The reason why we are good at our job is perhaps due to our inborn characteristics of loyalty and high standards.' It should be remembered that women were accustomed to hard work from an early age and their experiences provided them with the necessary strength and stamina required in their future lives as amahs.

Qualities such as honesty and reliability, besides being valued in China, were also essential attributes in their work as most jobs were obtained through personal recommendation. Without a reputation for honesty and reliability, jobs would have been difficult to come by; and the fact that most amahs belonged to sisterhoods strongly reinforced this as any default by one brought shame to the others.

Loyalty, their most highly regarded attribute, was due to a combination of several factors—upbringing, being abroad, and their single state. Though they enjoyed their independence, they missed some aspects of family life, particularly having their own children. Hence, they transferred their emotions and loyalties to the families they served.

When considering their remarkable qualities, one sometimes tends to forget that they were ordinary women from humble origins and not super beings imbued with special powers. And it is this 'ordinariness' that makes them truly extraordinary.

The term 'outstanding' is usually accorded only to people who have succeeded in fields that are always in the public eye. Recognition is seldom, if ever, given to people in mundane, everyday jobs.

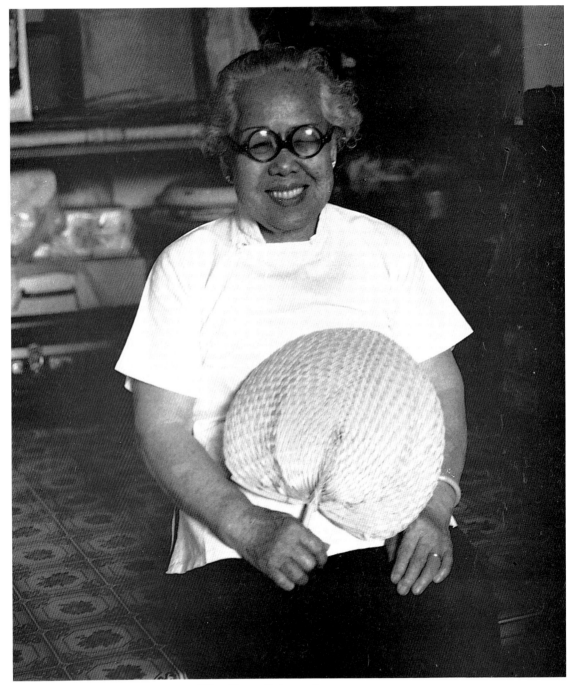

53 Wan Yong Gui, aged seventy-seven.

'... extraordinary women.'

(Photograph the author)

It should also be acknowledged that achievement is relative to circumstance. Had only one woman in pre-revolutionary China (before 1949) been able to live a life independent of men, it would have been nothing short of miraculous. That thousands of these illiterate Cantonese women of the Pearl River Delta managed not only to lead independent lives, but also to become the very best in their chosen profession of domestic service, make it an achievement without parallel.

They will long be remembered—these extraordinary women—these superior servants.

GLOSSARY

Amah	阿媽	Chinese female domestic servant.
Chai tong	齋堂	Vegetarian House.
Chi fun	煮飯	Cook.
Chi ka kung	住家工	'Family work' or domestic service.
Chi mui	姊妹	Women who have pledged to treat each other as 'sisters'.
Chi mui fong	姊妹房	'Sisters'' room; term for amahs' accommodation used in Hong Kong.
Chow tsai	湊仔	Baby amah or amah who looks after children.
Coolie fong	咕喱房	Workers' room; term for amahs' accommodation used in Singapore.
Fong tsai	房仔	Small room; term for amahs' accommodation used in Malaya.
Hong pau	紅包	'Red packet'—monetary gift in a red packet or envelope.
Kit Paai Chi Mui	結拜姊妹	Sworn-sisters Group.
Kongsi fong/uk	公司房／屋	Shared room/house; term for amahs' accommodation used in Malaya and Singapore.
Ku por uk	姑婆屋	Grand-aunts' or Old Maids' House.
Kung yan	工人	Working person; term used by the amahs to describe their occupation.

170

Lai see	利是	'Lucky money'—a term usually used instead of *hong pau* in Hong Kong.
Ma cheh	媽姐	Most commonly applied to women from the Shun Tak district who are servants and have taken vows of celibacy.
Mui tsai	妹仔	Girl domestic slave/servant.
Nui yan uk	女人屋	Girls' House.
Sai tong	洗燙	Amah who does the washing and ironing.
Sor hei	梳起	Literally, 'comb-up'; the taking of vows of celibacy.
Sui haak	水客	Literally, 'water guest'; a man who organized the amahs' travel arrangements and accompanied them abroad from China—usually a sailor, ex-sailor or trader.
Sup Chi Mui	十姊妹	Ten-sister Group.
Ta chup	打雜	Amah who does the laundry and cleaning.
Ta foo tau	打斧頭	Practice of making a profit on the marketing.
Yat keok tek	一腳踢	Literally, 'one-leg-kick'; amah who does all the household jobs.

TRANSLITERATION CHART

PLACES

Wade-Giles	**Hanyu Pinyin**	
Amoy	Xiamen	厦門
Anhwei	Anhui	安徽
Canton	Guangzhou	廣州
Chekiang	Zhejiang	浙江
Chong San	Zhongshan	中山
Fukien	Fujian	福建
Hunan	Hunan	湖南
Kiangsi	Jiangxi	江西
Kiangsu	Jiangsu	江蘇
Kwangsi	Guangxi	廣西
Kwangtung	Guangdong	廣東
Nam Hoi	Nanhai	南海
Ningpo	Ningbo	寧波
Poon Yue	Panyu	番禺
Sam Sui	Sanshui	三水
San Wui	Xinhui	新會
Shanghai	Shanghai	上海
Shun Tak	Shunde	順德
Swatow	Shantou	汕頭
Toi Shan	Taishan	台山
Tung Koon	Dongguan	東莞

BIBLIOGRAPHY

Government Sources

Census of British Malaya, 1921, 1931, 1947.
Hong Kong Annual Report of the Commissioner of Labour, 1946-47, 1947-48, 1948-49.
Report of the Commission on Mui Tsai in Hongkong and Singapore, London, HMSO, 1937.
Straits Settlements Blue Book, 1901, 1911.

Books and Articles

AYSCOUGH, FLORENCE, *Chinese Women Yesterday and Today*, London, Jonathan Cape, 1938.

BAKER, HUGH D. R., *Chinese Family and Kinship*, New York, Columbia University Press, 1979.

BUCKLEY, C. B., *An Anecdotal History of Old Times in Singapore*, reprinted Singapore, Oxford University Press, 1984.

CHEN TA, *Emigrant Communities in South China*, Shanghai, Kelly & Walsh, 1939.

CUSACK, DYMPHNA, *Chinese Women Speak*, reprinted London, Century Hutchinson Ltd., 1985.

ENDACOTT, G. B., *A History of Hong Kong*, London, Oxford University Press, 1958.

FAIRBANKS, JOHN KING, *Trade and Diplomacy on the China Coast*, Cambridge, Mass., Harvard University Press, 1964.

FREEDMAN, MAURICE, *Chinese Family and Marriage in Singapore*, London, HMSO, 1957.

GILLINGHAM, PAUL, *"At the Peak" Hong Kong between the Wars*, Hong Kong, Macmillan Publishers Ltd., 1983.

HORN, PAMELA, *The Rise and Fall of the Victorian Servant*, Gloucester, Alan Sutton Publishing, 1986.

KINGSTON, MAXINE HONG, *The Woman Warrior*, reprinted London, Pan Books Ltd., 1981.

LAI, T. C. (ed.), *Things Chinese*, Hong Kong, Swindon Book Co., 1979.

LANG, OLGA, *Chinese Family and Society*, New Haven, Yale University Press, 1946.

LATOURETTE, KENNETH SCOTT, *The Chinese—Their History and Culture*, 4th ed., New York, Macmillan, 1960.

___, *A History of Modern China*, reprinted Middlesex, Penguin Books Ltd., 1956.

LEBRA, JOYCE AND PAULSON, JOY, *Chinese Women in Southeast Asia*, Singapore, Times Books International, 1980.

LETHBRIDGE, H. J., *Hong Kong: Stability and Change*, Hong Kong, Oxford University Press, 1978.

MACNAIR, HARLEY FARNSWORTH, *Modern Chinese History*, Shanghai, Commercial Press Ltd., 1923.

McKIE, RONALD, *Malaysia in Focus*, London, Angus & Robertson Ltd., 1963.

MOORE, DONALD AND MOORE, JOANNA, *The First 150 Years of Singapore*, Singapore, Donald Moore Press Ltd., 1969.

PURCELL, VICTOR, *The Chinese in Malaya*, reprinted London, Oxford University Press, 1967.

SAYER, G. R., *Hong Kong 1862-1919*, Hong Kong, Hong Kong University Press, 1975.

SCHURMANN, FRANZ AND SCHELL, ORVILLE (eds.), *Imperial China*, Middlesex, Penguin Books Ltd., 1967.

SMEDLEY, AGNES, *China Correspondent*, reprinted London, Pandora Press, 1984.

SNOW, LOIS WHEELER, *Edgar Snow's China*, London, Orbis Publishing, 1981.

SONG ONG SIANG, *One Hundred Years' History of the Chinese in Singapore*, reprinted Singapore, Oxford University Press, 1984.

STOKES, GWENNETH AND STOKES, JOHN, *Modern China and Japan—A Concise History*, London, Longman Group Ltd., 1970.

TAN, CECILIA, 'The Black and White', *New Straits Times Annual*, Kuala Lumpur, Berita Publishing, 1983.

TAN, THOMAS TSU-WEE, *Your Chinese Roots*, Singapore, Times Books International, 1986.

TOPLEY, MAJORIE, 'Chinese Women's Vegetarian Houses in Singapore', *Journal of the Malayan Branch of the Royal Asiatic Society*, Vol. XXVII, Part 1, May 1954.

TSAO HSUEH-CHIN AND KAO NGO, *A Dream of Red Mansions*, abridged version, Hong Kong, The Commercial Press, 1986.

WONG, C. S., *An Illustrated Cycle of Chinese Festivities in Malaysia and Singapore*, Singapore, Jack Chia-MPH Ltd., 1987.

WORSWICK, CLARK AND SPENCE, JONATHAN, *Imperial China Photographs 1850-1912*, London, Scolar Press, 1979.

Unpublished Works

HO IT CHONG, 'The Cantonese Domestic Amahs', Academic Exercise, Department of Social Studies, University of Malaya, 1958.

LIM JOO HOCK, 'Chinese Female Immigration into the Straits Settlements 1860-1901', Academic Exercise, Department of History, University of Malaya, 1952.

TANG CHEE-HONG, 'The Cantonese Women Building Labourers', Research Paper, University of Malaya, 1961.

INDEX

175